Treasures of the Kennel Club

*Paintings, Personalities,
Pedigrees and Pets*

Treasures of the Kennel Club

Paintings, Personalities, Pedigrees and Pets

First published in 2000
by The Kennel Club,
1-5 Clarges Street, London W1Y 8AB

©The Kennel Club 2000

British Library Cataloguing-in-Publication Data
A catalogue record of this book is available from the British Library.

ISBN 0 900890 14 2

Text set in 11pt Garamond and printed by Geerings of Ashford Limited,
Cobbs Wood House, Chart Road, Ashford, Kent TN23 1EP.

Contents

Biographical details of the authors

BERNARD J. HALL is co-editor with Valerie Foss of "Treasures of the Kennel Club". He has spent a lifetime in journalism, working first in the provinces and then for The Daily Telegraph and The Sunday Telegraph. He later became a senior lecturer in journalism on residential journalist courses at a college in Portsmouth before freelancing for a number of publications. With his wife he has been active in dogs both on the show scene and with working gundogs since the 1960s, subsequently combining his work and recreational activities by writing for the canine press. Since 1984 he has commentated at many dog events, including Crufts, and in 1995 was elected to the General Committee of the Kennel Club.

Photo: Marc Henrie

VALERIE FOSS, a well-known author of canine books, initiated the thinking behind "Treasures of the Kennel Club". She is a championship show judge, awarding Kennel Club challenge certificates in 31 breeds and judged the gundog group at Crufts in 1995. She is a best-in-show judge at championship shows and under her Elswood affix there have been 16 English Setter and Golden Retriever champions in Britain. She is president of the National Gundog Association and Manchester Dog Show Society and sits on the General Committee of the Kennel Club. Her research into early Golden Retriever history has produced exciting discoveries which have increased knowledge of the breed. She also enjoys gardening.

Photo: Marc Henrie

ROGER FRENCH, chief executive (secretary) of the Kennel Club, took up his post on July 3, 1995. He had trained and qualified as a mechanical engineer with the Hawker Siddeley group, moving to British European Airways in central management advisory services. During the previous 25 years he specialised in the service sector of the business and has also held senior management positions in transport, food services and, for ten years, in computer services. He is married with three daughters and commutes to the Kennel Club from his home in Wiltshire.

Photo: Marc Henrie

MERIEL E HATHAWAY, until retirement, was always involved with education, firstly as a teacher, then district superintendent of radiotherapy with clinical, administrative, teaching and examining responsibilities. Under the Melfricka affix, she owned six Golden Retriever show champions together with many other Kennel Club challenge certificate and reserve CC winners. In partnership with Denise Barney she also owned a breed best in show winning Cocker Spaniel, an American Cocker Spaniel show champion and a championship show group winner. She is a founder member of the Portuguese Water Dog Club of Great Britain, the Midland Golden Retriever Club and other Golden Retriever breed clubs. She was the first chairman of the Golden Retriever Breed Council and is approved to judge the gundog group.

Photo: Carol Ann Johnson

BRIAN LEONARD joined the Kennel Club in 1978 at a time when its registration system was struggling with changes which had started in 1976. During his 20 years on the staff he acquired an intimate knowledge of the registration system. In his last five years as external affairs executive, handling public relations, he experienced all aspects of the world of dogs both at home and overseas.

HELEN POLLITT was born in Shropshire and lived and worked in Manchester before joining the Kennel Club in London in January, 1996. In her role as marketing manager she is responsible for all aspects of marketing for the Kennel Club and its services

Photo: David Paton

MICHAEL J R STOCKMAN is a retired veterinary surgeon who is now a trustee of the Kennel Club after having served as an elected member of its General Committee for 22 years. He is committed to assisting with the improvement of the overall standard of dog care and, as chairman of the Kennel Club Charitable Trust, is concerned with grants to aid research into dog-orientated projects. He has frequently written articles for the canine and veterinary press and has contributed to books on canine matters. He owns Keeshonds and a German Short-Haired Pointer and judges both at championship and open level.

Photo: David Dalton

Photo: Marc Henrie

ZENA THORN ANDREWS showed her first Irish Wolfhound in 1967. He went on to become the top dog for four years. Since then she has added 20 champion Irish Wolfhounds to 60 Miniature Wirehaired Dachshund champions. She is still breeding and showing with great success. Well over 500 Kennel Club challenge certificates have been awarded to her affix, Drakesleat. Zena is an all-round judge, judging regularly all over the world. She has an extensive collection of dog books and is interested in the origins and work of pedigree breeds and serves on the Kennel Club Breed Standards and Stud Book sub-committee.

Photo: E. Smethurst

NICK WATERS has been involved in the dog world since the late 1950s and has bred challenge certificate-winning Irish Water Spaniels, Mastiffs and a Standard Poodle. With Liz Waters, he shares the Zanfi affix. The kennel has been responsible for some of the top-winning IWS in Britain as well as other successful dogs world-wide. He gives Kennel Club challenge certificates in the gundog and working groups and has judged overseas in Scandinavia, Europe, Pakistan and America. He is a canine art historian and freelance writer with two dog books to his credit and is a contributing author to others. He regularly has articles published in magazines in England and America and on an occasional basis in other countries.

Photo: Liz Waters

BARBARA WALKER was born in Lancashire, studied for a degree in Information Studies at Birmingham Polytechnic and worked in the library of the Royal Botanic Gardens, Kew, during the sandwich year of her course. In 1989 she returned to the North as an assistant librarian for Lancashire College of Nursing, based in the centres of Preston and Blackpool, until 1995 when she joined the Kennel Club. She became a chartered librarian in 1993. Although she now lives in central London she had a country upbringing surrounded by horses, cats and a wide variety of dog breeds.

Photo: Marc Henrie

HRH Prince Michael of Kent with his Labrador Retrievers

Treasures of the Kennel Club

The last definitive work on the history of the Kennel Club was written in 1905. Its author, Edward William Jaquet, the then secretary of the Club, traced the first quarter of a century of the founding and growth of the club he served.

Much thought was given to compiling an updated volume in the same vein, but the present General Committee of the Club decided that instead of such a complete history something less formidable could be produced and the idea of "Treasures of the Kennel Club" was born. The co-editors gathered together a number of people to aid them, each of whom was asked to write a chapter on a specific aspect of the Club. The major section was the chapter dealing with the paintings, trophies and furniture owned by the Club, in every sense treasures. Other chapters relate to the various achievements of which the Club can be proud, such as the founding of its junior organisation and its attitude towards responsible dog ownership.

All of these treasures find a place in this book which, I am sure, will go a long way towards filling the gap which existed after Jaquet.

Michael

Preface

Nearly a century has passed since the work of the Kennel Club was written in detail. When they discussed a proposal for a new up-to-date history members of the General Committee soon realised that it was going to prove extremely costly and be an all-consuming effort for any one person.

So Valerie Foss suggested to me that perhaps the solution was a book written not by one person, or even two, but by a succession of authors each with his or her own chapter(s), the whole to be moulded into a single volume to be known as "Treasures of the Kennel Club". This concept was approved by the General Committee and with little further delay we set about inviting people to contribute.

It was soon apparent that the treasures in the truest sense of the word were those artefacts owned by the Kennel Club, the paintings, the trophies, the furniture and other solid demonstrations of material possessions. So this became the chapter around which all else was to evolve.

With that in place Mrs Foss and I concluded that other treasures lay in the men and women who, over the years, had formulated and shaped the growth of the club into what we have today. But without premises little could have been achieved, so we decided to include the various homes which have been occupied by the Kennel Club.

Then, of course, all else seemed to follow: the activities in which the Kennel Club has engaged over its 127 years of existence to the present time; the emergence of new activities in which dog lovers could share; and the rules needed to govern these activities, with such rules coming under constant revision to meet new and changing situations.

Those who have written this book are acknowledged on another page but there have been so many more who have contributed by producing research material, by recalling events within their lifetime, some stretching back many decades, not the least of whom has been Sir Dudley Forwood. Mrs Foss and I spent two interesting days talking with Sir Dudley and he provided many tales of life over the years at the Kennel Club, spanning his time as both a General Committee member and chairman of Crufts to the time when he was elected a vice president. Not all could be repeated within the covers of this book.

The Kennel Club is an ongoing target for criticism, often from those who do not appreciate the hard work which goes on behind the scenes but who rate the club by the costs imposed for its many services. Perhaps this book may remedy some of the misconceptions.

Not every activity has been granted space in the pages which follow. No mention has been made of the Kennel Club Charitable Trust set up in the early 1990s by the late chairman, Mr John MacDougall. This is not a philanthropic charity which doles out cash to help people meet the cost of veterinary bills. There are other charities which do this.

Rather it helps fund research and, on occasion, donates all or part of the finance needed for building and equipment at veterinary centres or rescue homes. The Charitable Trust is supported by the Kennel Club but is not a part of the Kennel Club in the sense that it is not accountable to any Kennel Club committee and its work is in the hands of five trustees. Incidentally, the Charitable Trust devotes its effort purely to the welfare of the dog and not to other animals, but relates the welfare of the dog to that of humans and research into the one often helps research into the other.

Neither does this book mention the disciplinary powers of the Kennel Club yet there is a committee whose responsibility is to hear complaints which may be referred to it and deal with them accordingly. Yet, strangely enough, the need for a Kennel Club arose in part because there were so many matters which needed to be controlled; shenanigans, if you like, which were bringing the whole business of owning and competing with dogs into disrepute.

Many hours have been spent by the various authors in researching and writing their chapters. Photographs have been collected from many sources. Mrs Foss has attended kindly to much of the pictorial content of the book while I have tried to marry the conflicting styles of writing into a cohesive whole.

It is hoped that this book will go some way towards repairing the failure of anyone to record in collected form in one volume events which have fashioned the growth of the Kennel Club since 1905 when the one and only history of the Kennel Club was published.

Bernard J Hall

*This map identifies the ten London homes of the Kennel Club
since it was founded in 1873*

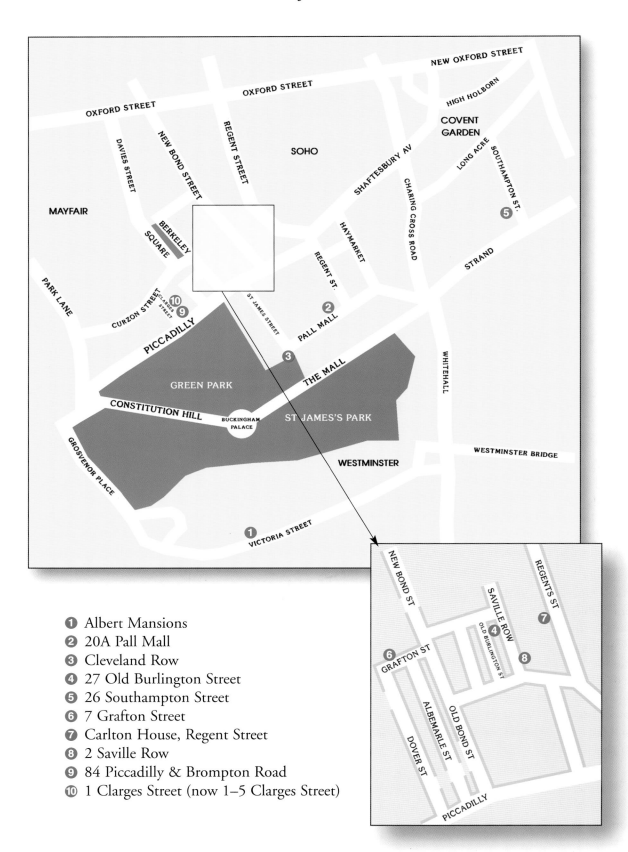

1. Albert Mansions
2. 20A Pall Mall
3. Cleveland Row
4. 27 Old Burlington Street
5. 26 Southampton Street
6. 7 Grafton Street
7. Carlton House, Regent Street
8. 2 Saville Row
9. 84 Piccadilly & Brompton Road
10. 1 Clarges Street (now 1–5 Clarges Street)

The Kennel Club began in modest style

THE reasons why The Kennel Club was formed are well chronicled in this volume, so suffice to say that unscrupulous and irregular practices resulted in many of the early dog shows going into bankruptcy. Thus it was that Mr. Sewallis Evelyn Shirley, MP, together with a few enthusiasts, started a controlling body. The irregularities which had been prevalent convinced the founders of the Kennel Club of the need to eradicate fraud and cheating in order to ensure fair play.

The new authority was first housed in modest accommodation in a small three-roomed apartment in Albert Mansions, Victoria Street, London, SW1. Having researched the *London Street Directory,* it was found that the premises were shared with one John Edward Shand, a wine merchant.

One of the club's first tasks was the production of a stud book containing the pedigrees of over 4,000 of the main winners during the previous 14 years. The book also contained Rules for the guidance of Shows and Field Trials. The first had ten rules and the latter 11. In comparison with today (127 years later) and the Kennel Club's present *Year Book,* it is obvious that progress has been made!

Gradually, but inexorably, the unaccepted practices experienced at the early dog shows became subject to discipline. There was no respite for any offender and the sport of showing dogs acquired a more respected status within the community. This more conducive state of affairs was maintained so that the breeding of dogs for sport and exhibition purposes became a fashionable hobby or pursuit, and it is a tribute to the continuance of the high standard achieved that it attracted the participation of Royalty. In succession to Edward VII, the ruling monarchs have graced the Kennel Club with their patronage.

From the premises in Albert Mansions, the Kennel Club moved to 29A Pall Mall, London, SW1 in 1877. Some six years later in 1883, the Kennel Club again moved, to 6 Cleveland Row, St James's, London, SW1. While the exact date of the next move is somewhat uncertain, research indicates that the Kennel Club moved to 27 Old Burlington Street, London, W1 in 1895.

Sunday 11th May, 1941. 1, 2 and 3 Clarges Street destroyed by bombing, with the Kennel Club then sited at 84 Piccadilly (in the background), which sustained only minor damage.

The main reason for these moves was the rapid growth in Kennel Club activities. It is interesting to note that the inception of the Kennel Club registry in 1880 provoked considerable protest. Not least of the antagonists was *The Field,* which, afterwards, became a firm supporter of the Kennel Club. What would happen, posed *The Field,* if 100,000 dogs were registered in a year? The task, they agreed, of dealing with such a number would be impossible. What would they have said about the 258,000 dogs registered in 1998?

Initially, registration was not compulsory before a dog could be shown. For some years, two classes of show ran side by side - those held under Kennel Club Rules, and unrecognised shows, which were not subject to authority of any kind. Clearly, as most people involved in the sport were aware, this situation was most unsatisfactory and detrimental to the interest of exhibitors. It was a common thing for unrecognised shows to default in payment of prize money, or to expect exhibitors to accept a reduced purse. In point of fact, promoters did pretty much as they pleased and, while some were reputable, most were not. At an extraordinary general meeting of the Kennel Club in 1904, it was proposed and carried that all shows should be brought under Kennel Club Rules. By this time, the Kennel Club had undertaken a further two moves - in 1900 to 26 Southampton Street, The Strand, London, WC2 and then to 7 Grafton Street, off Old Bond Street, London, W1 in 1902.

It might be interesting to pause here to read what was published in the *Kennel Gazette* of May 1901.

84 Piccadilly June 1953, decorated for the Coronation of the Kennel Club's Patron HM Queen Elizabeth II.

"There is general consensus of hearty approval at the impending migration of the Kennel Club from the precincts of Covent Garden. After we published the imminent possibility last month we were inundated with letters from incredulous ladies and gentlemen members (mostly the former) asking for confirmation of the good news. We were able to assure our correspondents that their days "among the cabbages" were numbered. Nobody is more pleased than ourselves and a habitation for the club nearer clubland will be all the better from every point of view."

John Bright once described England as the "Mother of Parliaments" so it may be claimed that the Kennel Club is the "mother of kennel clubs". It was not appreciated so early on how immensely important the Kennel Club would become alongside the tremendous growth in the breeding and exhibiting of the dog. And so it was that the Kennel Club moved yet again, in 1910, into a temporary office at, firstly, Carlton House, Regent Street, London, W1 and then, in 1911, to 2 Savile Row, London, W1. From its temporary office, and in the middle of the Great War 1916, the Kennel Club moved into

84 Piccadilly, London, W1 where, for 44 years, it consolidated its position in the world of dogs. A most distinctive landmark on Piccadilly was the Kennel Club Hound. At first the hound was sited in the bay window of the smoking room. Unfortunately, a club custom evolved in which members' ribald comments on the then personalities of the dog world were attached to those parts of the dog's anatomy that they considered suitable. The hound was therefore re-sited to the porch and for 27 years gazed across Piccadilly and into Green Park.

During this period the Kennel Club's activities continued to grow and additional office space was taken in Brompton Road, London, SW10 sometime around 1946/47. An opportunity arose in 1956 to acquire the freehold of 1-4 Clarges Street which was a bomb site and the General Committee of the day showed great foresight in purchasing the property in 1957, and even greater foresight in acquiring the freehold of 5 Clarges Street in 1964.

Although not strictly homes occupied by the Kennel Club in the sense in which we perceive them in this chapter, there are two other places which must be mentioned. One is the new home at Aylesbury for the Kennel Club registration department.

Functional rather than salubrious, this building was taken over by the Kennel Club during the summer of 1999 for its PetLog operation as well as registration. PetLog is the highly successful national pet identification scheme run by the Kennel Club.

The new home for these two operations is part of an early 1990s development built in red brick some 15 minutes walk from the centre of the town. The premises are fully air conditioned, something which has been yearned for in the current Clarges Street property for years. Readers should feel for all those members, committee members and staff who have to work in the Mayfair premises where summer temperatures can reach phenomenal heights.

Alton House, Aylesbury, was obtained on a ten-year lease and though some staff transferred from the London headquarters of the Kennel Club many others were recruited locally.

The other "home" of the Kennel Club is housed in an impressive building near Newmarket, Suffolk, and is, of course, the John MacDougall Visitor Centre at the Animal

Architect's proposal for 1 – 4 Clarges Street drawn by J Adams for S N Cooke & Partners (undated)

The Kennel Club offices in Aylesbury housing the Registration Department, July 1999.

The Kennel Club's permanent exhibition in the John MacDougall Visitor Centre at the Animal Health Trust opened by HRH Princess Anne in June 1998.

Health Trust, Lanwades Park, in what was formerly the stabling for Lanwades Hall.

The premises were built around 1900 and are Grade II listed. More recently, before its conversion, the building was used as the Animal Health Trust's estate yard with stores and a staff flat. The transformation work to turn it into a visitors' centre began in 1997 and the project cost £500,000. Much of the funding came from a supporter of the Animal Health Trust and friend of the late John MacDougall and it was requested it should be created in memory of the man who steered the Kennel Club through some difficult years between 1981 and 1996.

John MacDougall had strong connections with Lanwades for he had served on the council of management of the Animal Health Trust and was a member of its executive committee.

A portrait of him is in the exhibition area which shows the work of both the Kennel Club and the Trust.

Given the pace of change, particularly in the area of technological advance, who knows what lies ahead? One thing is highly likely and that is the Kennel Club will continue to prosper and adapt to change in relation to the obvious importance of the dog in society.

Roger French

Art — an insight to the pedigree dog

*T*O *understand* the development of art over the centuries is to understand the great changes which have taken place in society. The appreciation of any collection can be achieved only in the context of change; so it must be with the Kennel Club's collection, the largest of its kind in Europe.

The collection gives us an insight into the evolution of the pedigree dog, the characters who brought about this evolution and the artists who have recorded it. It stems from the days when dogs were kept solely for a purpose - usually pitted against another animal in one form or another; the arrival of early shows, or leads as they were sometimes called; the direct result of anti-cruelty legislation in the 1830's; the establishment of a Kennel Club and the keeping of records; organised shows and trials; fixing type in 'old' breeds and on to the creation of 'new' breeds.

The artists who have depicted these changes remind us of the various ways in which we have taken the dog into our lives: from sport to satire, self-grandiosity to companionship and even exploitation. We have given dogs human characteristics, they have even taken the place of humans and the Kennel Club's collection shows us all of this. Importantly, though, the collection shows us a new 'breed' of artist, one who has specialized in canine portraiture, which has endured in popularity for nearly 150 years.

The importance man has given to the dog is evident by the fact that it has appeared alongside him from the earliest civilisations. Dog and man were together in prehistoric cave paintings; in Egyptian, Greek and Roman art; throughout the Middle Ages and the Renaissance. The arrangement was not always an amicable one, but they stayed together. It was during the Renaissance period that the dog took on a more important role in art but the invention of the flintlock in c.1600 and the new English game laws introduced by Parliament in 1671, contributed greatly to the dog's

popularity in art and the emergence of the sporting artist.

Some of the earliest paintings in the collection show just how important dogs were to sport. For centuries falconry was THE sport and one which had its roots in the deserts of Arabia. In these Islands Scottish falconers were considered among the best, with the Flemings of Barochan Tower, Renfrewshire, being a family who passed down their skills, father to son for many generations.

James Howe's (1780-1836) painting of one of the family was completed about 1811 and shows Mr.Fleming seated on his horse with his hooded falcon on his fist *(Plate 1)*. With him is his falconer, the famous James Anderson, considered one of the last of the old Scottish falconers who was so celebrated as a falconer that the American naturalist, John James Audubon, paid him a special visit. Anderson's assistant, George Harvey and an assortment of dogs, including a small red and white Spaniel, a 'breed' depicted in falconry paintings since the 15th century and which many consider as the forerunner of the Welsh Springer are also featured. Interestingly, there is also a Poodle, a breed frequently included in Regency pictures to indicate a fop or a dandy.

An ancestor of Fleming received a hawk's hood set with jewels from James IV of Scotland, for beating the King's falcon with his Tiercel. James Howe was born in Sterling and died in Edinburgh but worked for a while in London as equine painter to George III.

By the middle of the 18th century, coursing had become the most popular of all sports and the collection houses two totally different paintings on the subject. The first is attributed to the North of England sporting artist John Ferneley, Jnr. (1815?-1862), considered less competent than his more successful father who also painted Greyhounds. The picture shows six dogs being released from their kennel by their keeper for exercise and it is interesting to note

Plate 1
James Howe (1780-1836).
Mr. Fleming with his
falconer, James Anderson,
one of the last of the old
Scottish falconers,
Anderson's assistant,
George Harvey, and an
assortment of dogs.
Oil on canvas. 20" x 25".

Plate 2
Henry Barraud
(1811-1874).
Beacon Hill Meeting,
October 1848.
Signed and dated 1853,
oil on canvas, 28" x 36".
An engraving of this
painting appeared as
the frontispiece to
The Greyhound by
Stonehenge.

Plate 3
English School. Bull-baiting or bull-running. c.1830, oil on canvas, 28" x 36".

that many of the sporting artists from this period and earlier, painted packs of Greyhounds as they did packs of hounds.

The second painting *(Plate 2)* shows two dogs at the end of a successful course, with a kennel boy and probably the owner and trainer. The mounted judge can be seen in the distance on a grey horse. Painted by a member of another family of sporting artists, Henry Barraud (1811-1874) grandson of Barraud the chronometer maker, the painting shows the Beacon Hill meeting in October 1848 and the two dogs are Brilliant and Leeway. It was engraved by E.Hacker and appeared as the frontispiece to *'The Greyhound'* by 'Stonehenge' first published in 1853.

Baiting sports were, for centuries, very popular and the English School study of three Bulldogs and a bull is an example of a once very popular theme in art. It shows Bulldogs of great courage and determination and very different to the type considered as ideal today. It is by the study of such pictures that one is able to appreciate just how certain breeds have changed and evolved.

Sometimes referred to as 'The Baited Bull Broke Loose' *(Plate 3)*, it could easily be a depiction of bull-running, a sport once popular

at Stamford in Lincolnshire and Tutbury in Staffordshire, for the bull is being pursued across a field by a group of followers. It could even be a depiction of bull-baiting in open country, for the sport was not confined solely to the bull-ring.

The Bulldogs are similar to Rosa and Crib of which the Kennel Club has an oil on copper after Abraham Cooper, R.A. (1787-1868). The original was painted in 1817 and in 1865 Philo-Kuon described Rosa as "nearly approaching perfection, in shape, make, and size of the ideal bulldog." She contrasts greatly to the plaster model which was considered 'The Perfect Bulldog' at the turn of the century *(Plate 4)*.

Plate 4
'The Perfect Bulldog' as supplied by Partridge Models Ltd. c.1900, plaster, 5³/₄" high.

Standing some 5 ³/₄" high, this was retailed by Partridge Models Ltd., Johnson St., Westminster and, in common with the practice of giving some materials a finish of that of a higher grade material, 'The Perfect Bulldog' has a bronze patination.

Following the banning of baiting and fighting sports, the rat pits came into their own. Jemmy (or Jimmy) Shaw's Queen's Head Tavern was

Plate 5
R. Marshall.
An Early Canine Meeting.
Signed and dated 1855,
oil on canvas, 29" x 37".
One of the most historic
of all dog paintings.

one of the most popular meeting points. He bought as many as 500 live rats each week and the livelihoods of whole Essex families were dependent upon the rats which Shaw bought from them. At times he would have as many as 2,000 live rats in his house. The dead carcases needed disposing of and every Wednesday morning the dustmen came and took these away.

In an age of matching one animal against another, dog shows were perhaps a natural progression and Shaw jumped at the opportunity to promote them. R.Marshall's painting 'An Early Canine Meeting' *(Plate 5)*, which was painted at Shaw's tavern in 1855 and which now hangs in the Kennel Club, is one of the most historic of all dog paintings. It shows Shaw and many of his regulars, all men and the majority smoking long clay pipes. A number of early breeds are shown; Bulldogs, Bull Terriers, Black and Tan Terriers but Toy Spaniels (although then divided by colour) make up the most of one breed. The walls are covered with prints depicting aspects of sporting life: cockfighting, ratting and boxing. Shaw himself

was a noted pugilist, being one of the most skilful light-weight boxers of his day.

The dogs at Shaw's and other such establishments were judged to a standard whereby type and certain points were paramount and such shows were the forerunners of the shows we know today. The ladies of the day had their own dog shows which were held in considerably more genteel surroundings and again the Toy Spaniel was the most popular breed. At these shows, always held in the afternoon, it was obesity which was the deciding factor.

One of the prints on the wall of Shaw's tavern depicts the famous Billy and an early print of Billy is also in the Kennel Club. *(Plate 6)* An advertising broadsheet for the Westminster Pit in March 1825 billed Billy as 'The Phenomenon of the Canine Race, and Superior Vermin Killer of his day having killed nearly 4,000 Rats in about Seven Hours.'

With the formation of the Kennel Club there came, also, keeping of records and breeding dogs for type rather than just for a purpose. The

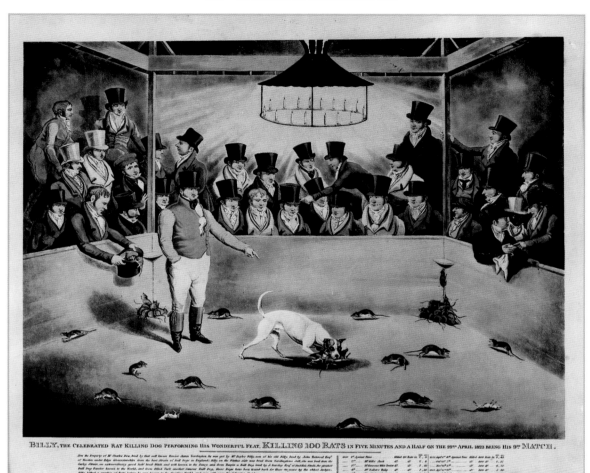

BILLY, THE CELEBRATED RAT KILLING DOG PERFORMING HIS WONDERFUL FEAT, KILLING 100 RATS IN FIVE MINUTES AND A HALF ON THE 22ᴺᴰ APRIL 1823 BEING HIS 9ᵀᴴ MATCH.

Plate 6
'Billy' coloured engraving
13¹/₂ x 17¹/₂.
Billy, the celebrated rat killing dog, was owned by Mr. Charles Dew and the engraving records the dog performing his wonderful feat, killing 100 rats in five minutes and a half on the 22nd April 1823, this being his ninth match.
The timekeeper can be seen on the right.

Plate 7
George Armfield
(1810-1893).
Terriers at a Rabbit Hole.
Oil on canvas, 28" x 36".
This painting shows the forerunners of some of today's terrier breeds.

9

second half of the 19th century saw the creation of many 'new' breeds of dogs. These 'new' breeds were from dogs of the sort artists like George Armfield (1810-1893), Edward Armfield - no relation - (op.c.1864-1875) and Paul Jones (op.1855-1888) recorded on canvas. These artists were prodigious and many of their paintings repeated a standard formula, nevertheless their work contributes to our understanding of how breeds evolved. George Armfield Smith (he never used Smith) was the more accomplished of the three and his work was exhibited at the Royal Academy and other galleries. Born at Monmouth, most of his life was spent in London where he kept his own private zoo. He enjoyed all sports and was a fine horseman whose life-style was reminiscent of the Regency Squire, Mad Jack Mytton. He rode one of his horses over lit bonfires and had one dance to music in front of Horse Guards. His painting of Terriers in the Kennel Club's

collection *(Plate 7)* shows clearly the forerunners of some of today's successful breeds in the showring.

One of the best known paintings in the collection is 'Buy A Dog Ma'am' *(Plate 8)* by Richard Ansdell,R.A. (1815-1885). Ansdell was one of the finest animal painters of the 19th century and the only British artist to have had a town named after him - Ansdell in Lancashire. Much of his work shows the influence of the great master of Victorian animal painting, Sir Edwin Landseer, R.A. (1802-1873) and many of his paintings were exhibited, including this one which was exhibited at the Royal Academy in 1860, the year in which it was painted. It is a great social document of the period showing the dejection of the working dogs, the toy dogs acceptance of the situation, the totally apathetic street-seller, the curiosity of youth and looking at the wares a somewhat distant young lady who

Plate 9
Sir Edwin Landseer, RA.
(after) (1802-1873).
'Ta Ageur'.
Hand coloured engraving
published by W. Schaws,
New York, 1852.
20" x 24".
The Poodle belonged to
Lady Williams.

would have no real knowledge, or even wish to, of the true plight of the dogs being offered for sale.

At the time this picture was painted, selling animals in the streets had become very profitable and was frequently a public nuisance. Street-sellers of dogs were often divided into those who sold 'fancy pets' and those who sold 'sporting dogs'. There were street-sellers of every conceivable animal from snails to hedgehogs to parrots and their total takings in a year in London alone were estimated at over £23,000. Street-sellers of 'sporting dogs' would take in the region of £12,000 and those selling 'fancy pets' £9,000.

Landseer was a favourite painter with Queen Victoria and his contribution to the dog in art is immeasurable. Although the Kennel Club does not have an original Landseer it does have a print of one of his paintings which he completed in 1821 when he was nineteen years old. It shows a harlequin Poodle belonging to Lady Williams. Entitled 'Ta Ageur' *(Plate 9)*, the dog is shown on a rocky seashore with rolling waves beyond. The print was engraved by Robt. Mitchell in 1852 and published the same year by W. Schaws, Southern District of New York.

The Victorian era was a great period for students of art to copy the works of great masters as part of their artistic training and the works of Edwin Landseer were much copied. One such hangs in the Kennel Club and is a copy of one of Landseer's best known works, the original of which hangs at Chatsworth having been bought by the 6th Duke of Devonshire.

'Laying Down The Law' (also called Trial by Jury) was painted in 1840 and exhibited at the Royal Academy the same year. The Poodle represents one owned by Count 'D'Orsay, the dog being in the habit of resting on a table in the attitude represented by Landseer and the idea for the painting came about after a certain Lord commented that "the animal would make a capital Lord Chancellor." The judge in question represented by the Poodle has been identified as Lord Brougham. According to Richard Ormond in *Sir Edwin Landseer* "The unlikely combination of breeds and the exaggerated expressions of the individual dogs draw out the uneasy humour and satire of the courtroom scene." The Toy Spaniel behind the Greyhound was the Duke of Devonshire's dog Bony, who was inserted after the other dogs and

Arthur Wardle
(1864-1949).
Headstudy of a tricolour
King Charles Spaniel.
The purchase was made
in accordance with the
policy of complementing
The Kennel Club's
collection of paintings
with breeds not previously
represented. Prior to its
purchase it had been in
the collection of dogs in
art formed by Count
Alarico Palmieri. Signed,
oil on canvas,
21" x 15'.

11

after the etching by Thomas Landseer was published in c.1841-42.

Casting animals in the role of humans and giving them human personalities and sentiments was nothing new. Cartoonists and satirists had been doing it for generations. It reached its height of popularity in the late 19th century and recently it has seen a revival. Frank Paton's (1856-1909) 'The Card Game' which he painted in 1885 is typical of this anthropomorphic approach in art *(Plate 10)*. Paton exhibited regularly at the Royal Academy until 1890 when he had a dispute with the organisers which prevented him exhibiting thereafter. Today he is perhaps known best for his genre illustrations with their remarqued borders but he was capable of highly finished work as the card game shows. One's social standing was never far from the surface, even in art, and the cat, whose social status would be less than that of the dog's, looks on very questioningly at the Poodle who has just won a hand. The Pug also has some doubts but the Toy Spaniel, Yorkshire Terrier and the broken coated terrier accept the inevitable.

'The Card Game' and 'Buy A Dog Ma'am' are two of the most important paintings in the

Kennel Club's collection and along with Mr.Fleming and His Falconers and the copy of Landseer's 'Laying Down The Law', were presented to the Club by the late Hon.Mrs.Nellie Ionides. Mrs.Ionides was a daughter of Admiral Lord Charles William de la Poer Beresford and was twice married, her second husband being the architect, Basil Ionides who rebuilt Buxted Park after a fire destroyed it. Her Vulcan Champagne kennel will forever be a household name in Standard Poodles and at its height she maintained a kennel of 100, nearly all in lion trim. There were also a few Sealyhams and one or two other breeds. She was passionate about art and her collection and was an authority on Bilston enamel, owning one of the most comprehensive collections. She bought regularly in The Pantiles at Tunbridge Wells, an old Victorian shopping centre where a lot of top of the range dealers had shops. She was so knowledgeable that some of the dealers would keep pieces back for her opinion.

For many years she served on the Ladies' Branch of the Kennel Club and gave the pictures to the Club in 1957 and at first they hung in the Dining Room. She died in 1962 but the Kennel Club were not represented at

*Plate 11
Attributed to Pieter Boel
(1622-1674). Two Dogs
with dead game. signed,
oil on canvas, 29" x 39".
The spotted dog is clearly
an early Dalmatian type.*

her memorial service. It is possible that she also gave to the Club the Landseer print and a number of the early 19th century satirical cartoons for they all include Poodles.

The oldest painting in the collection is attributed to Pieter Boel who was born in Anvers (Antwerp) in 1622 and died in Paris in 1674. Boel was noted for his studies of animals and still life. This painting *(Plate 11)* shows a spotted dog of early Dalmatian type together with a type of dog often depicted as an early retriever. By the Dalmatian's feet are dead game, indicating the sporting connection of the two dogs.

The painting was once part of a collection of Dalmatian art formed by Martin S.Fisher, one time General Committee member of the Club, and was presented to the Kennel Club by Mrs.Kathleen Fisher. It is the sort of painting which Fisher could well have bought from the late Gerald Massey, one of the Kennel Club members who represented the Club at Fisher's cremation at Golders Green Crematorium.

Gerald Massey was the first dealer to specialize in art and literature on the dog. He made people aware of this great heritage which existed and unquestionably saved many important pieces which otherwise would have

been lost forever. He started in business selling from a street barrow in Knightsbridge with general stock and a few dog books. A relative in Dublin helped him in his quest for stock. Massey later transferred his business to his home in Streatham. He became a member of the Club in 1946, being seconded appropriately by the great bibliophile, A.Croxton Smith. Massey was passionate about dog books, dog paintings and the Kennel Club, of which the latter played an important part in his life. It is possibly true to say that it also introduced him to some useful clients. His profession on his passport was originally given as 'bibliographer' but he managed to persuade the Foreign Office to have it changed to 'biblidographer' and it remained so until his death.

Tradition within the family has it that he gave the Kennel Club what is now one of their most valuable possessions. This is the large oil by John Emms (1843-1912) of nine of Sir Humphrey de Trafford's English Setters *(Plate 12)*. Certainly it was in the late Gerald Massey's possession in 1956 and hung in the hallway at his home. Sir Humphrey was an outstanding example of a large scale dog breeder of the 19th century who kept kennels of many breeds and who put the 'great' in great British

13

breeders. He was the 3rd Baronet and related to the Earls of Shrewsbury. Field trials, dog shows and breeding dogs were three of his interests listed in his entry in *Who's Who*. The dogs in Emms' painting are Barton Rap, Ch.Grouse of Kippen, Duchess of Welbeck, Ch.Mallwyd Bess, Barton Charmer, Barton Lucy, Barton Maud, Ch.Mallwyd Flo and Ch.Barton Tory. Rap and Charmer were second in the Kennel Club brace stake in 1896; Bess and Flo came from Tom Steadman's kennel which had been started with a bitch from a strain which had been kept for working purposes by his family long before dog shows; Tory was best of breed at Crufts in 1898 and '99 and was later owned by S.E.Shirley, founder of the Kennel Club, and G.Raper, before being sold to America.

Emms was born in Norfolk but lived the latter part of his life in the New Forest. He was the son of an artist and in his early years as an artist worked in London as a studio assistant to the Victorian neo-classical painter, Lord Frederick Leighton, the only English artist to have been elevated to the peerage. Emms, who exhibited work at most of the major galleries, developed a very distinctive style of bold brush strokes loosely applied and Sir Humphrey's Setters are an example of the very best of Emms' work.

Two other important works by Emms hang in the collection. These are studies of Borzois owned by Her Grace, Kathleen, Duchess of Newcastle (under-Lyme), first chairman of the Committee of the Ladies' Branch of the Kennel Club. In her will Her Grace bequeathed a number of trophies and paintings to the Club, including three large paintings by Emms of Borzois. At one time these were housed by the wife of a member of the Kennel Club, but the Club had difficulty in reclaiming its property and the fate of the third Emms is not known. Her Grace was the wife of the seventh Duke whose ancestors served under the Black Prince in France. She was the daughter of Major Henry and the Hon.Mrs. Candy and is remembered as much for her Fox Terriers as she is for her Borzois. Her home, Clumber Park, will be associated forever as being the spiritual home, if not the birthplace, of the Clumber Spaniel.

The Duchess's mother received a Borzoi bitch, appropriately named Spain, as a gift from the Marquis of Quadelmina and it was Spain's disposition and character that won over the then Kathleen Candy. Her first Borzoi was a dog named Ivan II, purchased in Paris at the French Kennel Club show in 1890. With her unlimited resources the Duchess went on to establish one of the greatest kennels of Borzois

Plate 13
John Emms (1843-1912).
Four of the Duchess of
Newcastle's Borzois.
Signed and dated 1892,
oil on canvas, 40" x 60".
The hounds are
Nagrajdai, Oudar,
Golub, and Ooslad.

Plate 14
Attributed to
William Frank Calderon
(1865-1943).
One of the paintings
bequeathed to
the Kennel Club by
her Grace, Kathleen,
Duchess of Newcastle. Oil
on canvas,
44" x 45".

in this country. She arranged for a Mr.Bless to visit Russia and he returned with a consignment of the best hounds available, including Ooslad. In 1892 no less than sixteen hounds were sent to London by The Tzar to be exhibited at Crufts, then held at the Agricultural Hall, Islington. After the show they were sold and the best of the hounds, Oudar, was bought by the Duchess for a reputed £200.

The Borzois featured in the two Emms paintings are Ch.Tsaretsa, bred by Gen.Boldariff; Ch.Milka, bred by Col.Tschesbishoff, the second champion in the breed in this country; the homebred Ch.Vikhra; Nagrajdai; Oudar; Golub, Ch.Vikhra's sire; and Ooslad. Oudar and Golub were very important foundation sires in the breed in this country and Ooslad also left his mark as a stud dog *(Plate 13 shows Nagrajdai, Oudar, Golub and Ooslad)*.

Another of the Duchess' bequests in the collection is a portrait of a Borzoi *(Plate 14)* attributed in her will to William Frank Calderon (1865-1943) who founded the School of Animal Painting in 1894 and whose first painting which he exhibited at the Royal Academy in 1881 was bought by Queen Victoria. The Borzoi painting may prove to be one of the unsolved mysteries of the collection.

A brass plaque beside the painting states that the hound is 'Ch.Vetch', but in her will the Duchess bequeaths 'the Borzoi Champion Velsh'. In fact there was no champion Borzoi of either name in this country, neither did the Duchess own one so named.

She did, however, own a famous dog named Ch.Velsk, the sixth Borzoi to become a champion and the sire of four champions, so on the surface it would appear that there has been a mix up of names, or a mistake on the part of a typist, and Velsk is in fact the dog in the painting. However, photographs of Velsk show a dog with entirely different markings to the dog in the painting. From the markings, Tsaretsa could be a contender.

There are only a few paintings in the collection which carry attributions, most either being fully signed or fully authenticated. One of the attributions is an oil on canvas attributed to William Hogarth (1697-1764). The painting shows the head of a Pug type dog, the Pug being one of the most featured of all breeds in art but poorly represented in the Kennel Club collection. Hogarth owned a dog called Trump and his self portrait with Trump is one of the best known of all paintings to include a dog. Although the Kennel Club painting carries an old plaque proclaiming the dog as being called

Plate 16
Maud Earl (1863-1943).
Mrs Greene's Welsh
Springer Spaniels,
Ch.Longmynd Myfanwy
and Ch.Longmynd
Megan.
Signed and dated 1906,
oil on canvas, 18" x 24".

Trump, it bears little resemblance to Hogarth's dog, being shorter in muzzle and having cropped ears. The balance of the Kennel Club's painting would suggest that the dog was once part of a much larger painting.

Although until 1979, ladies were not accorded full membership of the Kennel Club, it is thanks to many of the ladies who have been associated with the Club over the years that it has such an important and interesting collection of art. Had some of them not thought the surroundings of the Club rather drab, this may never have happened.

Four paintings of Pomeranians painted by Maud Earl (1863-1943) are four such decorative pictures. Earl was the daughter of the well known animal artist, George Earl, and is perhaps the artist most associated with the painting of pure bred dogs. Her list of patrons reads like a *Who's Who* of dogdom and included Edward VII and the aforementioned Duchess of Newcastle.

The paintings of the Pomeranians were commissioned by Lady Wavertree, then Mrs. Hall-Walker, who kept both Pomeranians exceeding 8lb and Pomeranians not exceeding 8lb, both breeds having challenge certificates

well into this century. One of the paintings is a study of three of her smaller ones, Ch.Dainty Boy, whose breeding is unknown, Ch.Gateacre Bilbury Belle, who soon went back to unregistered stock and their daughter, Ch.Gateacre Dainty Belle *(Plate 15)*. Mrs. Hall-Walker was one of the early admirers of the unfashionable shaded sable colour and Dainty Boy was only the second English champion of the colour.

The second picture also includes Dainty Belle together with Gateacre Lupino and Gateacre Philander and this painting is the original study for the photogravure 'Professional Beauties' which appeared in Maud Earl's portfolio of 'Terriers and Toys'. The third picture of Mrs. Hall-Walker's dogs shows Ginger Pop, registered in the exceeding 8lb register. His mother was an unregistered bitch named Spitz and his father was Prince Ginger whose pedigree is unknown. The fourth picture is of a dog whose identity is not known. It is interesting to note that Mrs. Hall-Walker, and many other breeders for that matter, established highly successful kennels on dogs of unknown parentage.

Her husband was Conservative M.P. for Widnes from 1900-1919 and was created first Baron Wavertree in 1919. He was a racehorse

17

owner who presented his stud of racehorses and mares to the nation in 1916 so as to start a National Stud.

Another successful dog breeder who was married to an M.P. was Mrs.Harriet Greene, whose husband was Henry Greene, Conservative M.P. for Shrewsbury from 1892-1900. He was also a former Governor of the Bank of England. Mrs.Greene was another of Maud Earl's patrons and a devotee of two Welsh breeds, the Springer and the Welsh Terrier. The painting of the Welsh Springers, Ch.Longmynd Myfanwy and her sister Ch.Longmynd Megan, was painted in 1906 *(Plate 16)* and is considered one of Maud Earl's finest pictures from this period and one of the best of her pictures in the Kennel Club's collection. Mrs.Greene's kennel dominated the breed until the First World War, when as a patriotic gesture to save food she had the whole kennel put down.

The painting of the Welsh Terriers, Ch.Longmynd Chamberlain and Ch.Longmynd Enchantress *(Plate 17)*, is another fine example of Maud Earl's work from this period. Chamberlain was out of her first Welsh Terrier, Ch.Cambrian Princess, who was from unregistered parents and Enchantress was out of

Brynhir Bride, bred in the famous kennel of W.S.Glyn and related to the famous Ch.Brynhir Ballad, who in 1902 was considered to be "the best Welsh Terrier of either sex that has ever appeared on the show bench." Among her many attributes she had "never been possessed of any of those parasites which so often are the bane of a dog's life."

The strength of the Kennel Club's collection lies in its Maud Earls of which the painting of the Rev.R.O'Callaghan's two Irish Setters, Ch.Shandon II and Ch.Geraldine II *(Plate 18)* is a fine example of her earlier more finished work. O'Callaghan had one of the most successful kennels in the breed and both Shandon and Geraldine were owner bred and their achievements were almost unique in the history of the breed at that time. Shandon was out of O'Callaghan's bitch, Grouse II, who was bred from the famous Palmerston, and in 1879 she was chosen to be the most typical Irish Setter. Maud Earl's painting was completed for the artist's first solo exhibition which was held at Messrs. Graves Galleries in Pall Mall, London in 1897. Seventy of her paintings hung in the exhibition and they represented 48 varieties of dogs, considered a staggering figure at that time. A reviewer of the exhibition described the

Plate 18
Maud Earl (1863-1943).
Rev. R. O'Callaghan's
Irish Setters,
Ch.Shandon II and
Ch.Geraldine II. Signed,
oil on canvas, 30" x 40".
This painting was one of
seventy in the artist's first
solo exhibition in 1897.

Plate 19
Maud Earl (1863-1943).
E. B. Joachim's Beagles,
Lonely II and Ch.Reader.
Signed and dated 1895,
oil on canvas, 25" x 30".
This painting is a fine
example of Maud Earl's
work from the mid
1890's.

Setters as "A subject picture, admirable not only as portraits, but for the life and animation which the painter has endued them."

Mr. O'Callaghan spent nearly 25 years at sea as a Royal Navy chaplain. He was elected to the Kennel Club Committee in 1884 and died on the 9th January 1897, days after attending the usual monthly meeting of the Club Committee.

The painting of the litter-mate Beagles Lonely II and Ch.Reader *(Plate 19)* is another fine example of Maud Earl's work from the mid 1890's. The two hounds were bred and owned by Mr.E.B.Joachim in 1892 and were by a dog named Rosewood, whose mother was a bitch named Primrose Countess. She was bred by George Krehl, who contributed greatly to the establishment of many breeds in this country. Reader was the most successful Beagle during the 1890s and was the first C.C. winner in the breed at Crufts in 1898, repeating his win in 1899. Maud Earl's picture of the two Beagles was bequeathed to the Kennel Club by Joachim in 1920. A pen and ink drawing in the collection by R.H.Moore dated '90 features Ch.Lonely and Primrose Countess.

Maud Earl's painting of Edwin Brough's three champion Bloodhounds *(Plate 20)* was painted in her studio which was then at Bloomfield Place, just off Bond Street, but the finished picture shows the hounds on a cliff top with the sea beyond, probably near Scarborough, where Brough had retired to live the life of a gentleman having made his fortune in the family's silk manufacturing business in Staffordshire. The hounds featured are Ch.Benedicta, Ch.Babbo and Ch.Barbarossa, the latter being the first C.C. winner in the breed at Crufts in 1897. Maud Earl described them as "very good sitters in the studio."

Brough's first appearance in the show-ring was in 1871 and he went on to establish one of the most successful kennels in the breed and his hounds made the head of the Bloodhound what it is. He helped formulate the Bloodhound standard and was responsible in no small part for the running of the Association of Bloodhound Breeders' first trials in October 1898. Such was his attention to detail that he saw to it that special trains ran from York to Robin Hood's Bay for the event.

One event in history which no doubt contributed to the Bloodhound's lasting popularity and with Brough being remembered,

Plate 21
Henry Rankin Poore,
American, (1859-1940).
Edwin Brough's Bloodhound,
Ch.Bardolph. Signed, oil on
canvas, oval, 21¹/₂" x 17¹/₂".
This painting is personally
inscribed to Brough.

was Jack the Ripper and the Whitechapel murders of 1888. Brough offered two hounds, Barnaby and Burgho, to Sir Charles Warren, the Commissioner of the Metropolitan Police, for tracking down the perpetrators of the murder to see if the hounds could succeed where Scotland Yard had failed.

Although successful trials were carried out in Hyde Park, when it came to the streets of London, the hounds were found to be useless. Brough insisted his hounds should be given more time, but added to the problems was the authority's reluctance to pay the insurance cover which Brough required. After a month the hounds were taken back to Scarborough by their owner without having been given a chance to track 'the Ripper'.

Among Brough's exports were dogs to America where they were exhibited and trialled with success. Some hounds were bred in America from stock sent out by Brough which recorded him as the breeder. Another painting of one of Brough's hounds *(Plate 21)* hangs in the Kennel Club, this being a head study by the American artist, Henry Rankin Poore (1859-1940). The hound featured is Ch.Bardolph, who at one show was described as being "one of

the finest young hounds seen for a long time." The painting is inscribed 'To my esteemed friend Edwin Brough Esq of Scarborough'. The hound could well have been one which helped establish Brough's type of Bloodhound in America but as there is no record of Bardolph in America, it is therefore more likely that the painting was a gift to Brough of a portrait of one of his favourite hounds.

The French Bulldog is the breed which has perhaps the most romantic history of all breeds. From the small runt Bulldogs taken to Normandy by the Nottinghamshire lace-makers, it became a favourite with the ladies of the night and the theatre people of Paris, and finally became the favourite with the crowned heads of the world and those who aspired to be crowned heads.

Hanging in the collection is Maud Earl's original study for the photogravure number 22 in her portfolio of 'Terriers and Toys'. Entitled 'Toy Bulldog. England Expects' it features Lady Pilkington's Ch.Peter Amos who stood 13" and weighed 19¹/₂lb and Ch.Ninon de L'Enclos who weighed 13lb. *(Plate 22)* Toy Bulldogs had challenge certificate status from 1896 until 1914 but did not survive the First World War.

Plate 22
Maud Earl (1863-1943).
Lady Pilkington's Toy
Bulldogs, Ch.Peter Amos
and Ch.Ninon de L'Enclos.
Signed, oil on canvas, 18"
x 24".
Lady Pilkington made up
eight of the twenty
champions in the breed.

Plate 23
Maud Earl (1863-1943).
F. Clegg's Irish Terrier,
Ch.Belfast Erin.
Signed and dated 1898,
oil on canvas, 25" x 30".
Erin is descended from the
celebrated Ch.Brickbat.

Plate 24
Arthur Wardle (1864-1949). 'The Totteridge XI'. signed and dated 1897, oil on canvas, 27¹/₂" x 35¹/₂". The dogs are l. to r. in the straw, Dryad, Ch.Daddy, Dame Dalby, Dalby (sitting) and Divorcee: standing foreground l. to r. Ch.Dominie, Ch.Donna Fortuna, Ch.Dame Fortune, Ch.D'Orsay, Ch.Donnington and Diamond Count. Reproduced with the permission of the Thomas Ross Collection.

Lady Pilkington made up eight of the 20 champions in the breed and she was one of two people who helped establish it. Describing her ideal Toy Bulldog, she wrote "he should be an exact replica of the big Bulldog, rose ears included ... bat ears have of late become the trademark of that strange animal, the 'French Bulldog', so called because it is neither French nor Bulldog!" It can be seen from Maud Earl's painting of Peter Amos that his ears were not his fortune. There was much political in-fighting between supporters of Toy Bulldogs, Miniature Bulldogs and French Bulldogs: the Kennel Club would not have them, the Bulldog people did not want them but the French Bulldog Club finally won the day and that breed survived, although all three were probably variants of the same.

Another painting by Maud Earl in the collection features the well known winning Irish Terrier bitch, Ch.Belfast Erin. *(Plate 23)* She was owned by F.Clegg and bred by Mr.McIlhagga in 1896 and was the winner of a number of CCs. She was by a dog named Milford Topper who was sired by the celebrated Ch.Brickbat, winner of the 60-Guinea Challenge Cup 12 times in succession, an unheard of record .

Other paintings by Maud Earl hanging in the collection are an oil dated 1912 of three Welsh Springers and a pair of canvases 46" x 18³/₄" showing Fox Terriers rabbiting. The terriers were bequeathed to the Kennel Club by Fox Terrier breeder, one time Vice-President of the Club and a former Director of the Bank of Scotland, J.S.Abbott JP. The pair of canvases are two of four, the others hanging in the collection of the American Kennel Club, and were probably intended to form a four panel screen.

The Fox Terrier is the most featured breed in the collection and from the many paintings, Arthur Wardle's (1864-1949) 'The Totteridge XI' is one of the most important and well known *(Plate 24)*. Wardle, along with Maud Earl, is one of the most highly regarded of the artists who specialised in dog portraiture. He had little formal training but studied live animals at London Zoo and his paintings of big cats are some of his best work.

'The Totteridge XI' is a classic example of dog portraiture and was executed under the ever watchful eye of Redmond, the dogs' owner. Many years after the completion of the picture, Wardle remarked: "Mr.Redmond stood over me and made me 'perfect' all his dogs - shorten

23

their backs, lengthen their necks and muzzles, make their ears and feet far smaller than they really were - and so on. None of them were half as good as in their picture."

Wardle was THE expert at painting what his patrons would want to see and his painting 'Field Spaniels of the 20th Century' is another prime example, some of the dogs showing little resemblance to their photographs taken around the same time.

'How's That Umpire?' or 'The Totteridge XI', was painted in 1898 and the title led many non-terrier or doggy people to believe that the XI referred to a North London cricket team! Redmond was Chairman of the Kennel Club from 1922-25 and by profession was a partner in a well-known firm in the City of London. He first became interested in the Fox Terrier as a sporting dog for rabbiting and underground work and purchased his first in 1869. Soon afterwards he had his first notable win in the show-ring, taking the cup for best Fox Terrier at Essex Agricultural Society's Show. He had many sporting interests and was at one time Field Master to a pack of Draghounds.

The dogs' featured in 'The Totteridge XI' are Dryad, Ch.Daddy, Dame Dalby, Dalby, Divorcee, Ch.Dominie, Ch.Donna Fortuna,

Ch.Dame Fortune, Ch.D'Orsay, Ch.Donnington and Diamond Count. Ch.Dominie was very important as a sire and his daughter, Ch.Donna Fortuna, was considered by most as the greatest example of a Smooth Fox Terrier that ever lived. She was shown consistently for five years and never defeated.

At the time of Charles Cruft's first show in 1891 the Smooth Fox Terrier was the most popular breed and B.O.B. at the first show was Ch.Dominie. In 1893 Ch.D'Orsay was first in the challenge class and hanging beside 'The Totteridge XI' is the framed Crufts Dog Show medal won by D'Orsay, although it has to be said that he was the only entry in the class. He did, however, go on to win the Crufts Challenge Cup valued at 15 guineas.

D'Orsay was bred by F.W.F. Toomer in July 1889 and originally registered Russley Toff and Redmond paid for him 200 guineas and for Dominie he paid 100 guineas. Among the many honours bestowed upon Redmond during well over 50 years in which he was involved with the breed, was judging the first specialty of the American Fox Terrier Club in 1885.

'The Totteridge XI', of which prints from the original were published by Fred Mansell, was

24

Plate 26
William Eddowes Turner
(c.1820-1885).
Fox Terriers at Newstead
Abbey. Label verso, oil on
canvas, 36" x 28".
Trimmer, the dog in the
foreground just to the
right of the rabbits, was
the first Fox Terrier to
win a prize at any British
dog show.

presented to the Kennel Club by Captain Tudor Crosthwaite in 1940 on behalf of Redmond's niece, Sarah Talbot. A later and slightly smaller version without the evidence of the artist's changes hangs in the offices of the American Kennel Club in New York. It was Tudor Crosthwaite who agreed to Wardle making a copy for the American Kennel Club and this was first hung in their offices in 1937. The then president of the American Kennel Club, Russell H.Johnson, said of the picture: "Were I to judge every picture we own, I would place it an easy first."

Wardle's brilliance as an artist was not matched by his ability to get dogs names correct when he gave inscriptions to his work. The Wardle picture in the collection inscribed by the artist 'D'orcy' could well be a preliminary study for D'Orsay as he appeared in 'The Totteridge XI'. Though facing in the opposite direction the dog is shown in the same stance.

Two other paintings by Arthur Wardle hanging in the collection feature Fox Terriers associated with Redmond. Both these were bequeathed to the Club by Neville Dawson. The first, 'Rival Beauties', was painted in 1901 and shows Ch.Donna Fortuna and Ch.Duchess of Durham. Duchess won the bitch C.C. at Crufts three years running and her sire, Durham, was Donna Fortuna's litter brother.

The second painting was completed in 1922 and features the half sisters, Ch.Dusky Dinah, sold to the Maharajah of Pithapuram, and Ch.Dusky Doris. *(Plate 25)* Their sire was Ch.Myrtus whom Redmond bought from Dr.Master, a successful breeder of noted terriers. Those who long for the return of prize money at shows may like to reflect on the £260 prize money which Redmond's team of dogs won at the Fox Terrier show in 1900, a phenomenal sum in those days. Upon Redmond's death in 1927 all the remaining terriers in his kennel were auctioned to raise funds for the Fox Terrier Club.

A painting of Fox Terriers in the collection historically more important to the breed than the 'The Totteridge XI' is William Eddowes Turner's (c.1820-1885) 'Fox Terriers at Newstead Abbey' *(Plate 26)*. Turner was a Nottingham based self-taught animal and sporting painter whose patrons included the 6th Duchess of Newcastle for whom this study of terriers with a view of Newstead Abbey beyond was painted. The painting shows 31 dogs at a transitional time for the breed when it was moving from being purely a hunt terrier to one of show dog as well.

A key to the painting identifies all the dogs, ancestors of the modern Fox Terrier. The dogs were hunt as well as show dogs and came from such hunts as the Grove, Oakley, Beaufort and Quorn. The dogs wearing collars were all prizwinners from 1862 onwards and include Trimmer (number 27, the dog in the foreground just to the right of the two rabbits) the first Fox Terrier to win first prize at any British dog show, Islington 1862.

The painting was purchased by the Kennel Club in 1994 from John Williams of Herefordshire for £7,000, it having passed to him through the family by descent. It is interesting to note the length of each dog's tail, the longer length being preferred by terrier men, as the dogs were easier to locate and extract from earths, therefore saving a lot of digging. They have the length of tail that Parson Jack Russell preferred. The parson was a friend of the Williams family, a great hunting family, and he baptised John Williams' grandmother. On handing the child back to her mother he commented: "I have christened her with Holy water, you see she is blooded by the age of twelve."

Redmond's Terriers and those of Robert Vicary, JP were related, with Redmond's Ch.Duchess of Durham going directly back to a number of dogs owned by Vicary. They were at one time great rivals in the show ring but Redmond ultimately won the war. John Emms' reputation frequently rests on his portraits of hounds and terriers and his painting of Vicary's Vesuvienne which hangs in the collection is typical of his output. Vicary purchased his first dog for 15 shillings and exhibited at a show in Devon under Parson Jack Russell in 1870. He was a charter member of the Fox Terrier Club and is also recorded in the Kennel Club Stud Books as owning Toy Terriers (Smooth Coated). Vesuvienne was considered as one of his more notable Fox Terriers.

Another Emms Fox Terrier painting in the collection is the more accomplished portrait of Brockenhurst Dame, a granddaughter of Redmond's Ch.D'Orsay. Dame was owned by J.C.Tinne, JP who successfully bred Fox Terriers for more than 40 years. It was Tinne who in 1899 proposed that the office of President be established at the Kennel Club and that Mr.Shirley be asked to accept the honour upon his resignation as chairman. This was passed at a special general meeting on 27th March .

May Reeks (exh.1909-10) was a Christchurch based artist who exhibited at the Royal Society of Artists, Birmingham, and at the London Salon. She was married to the Fox Terrier breeder, F.Reeks and an oil of his Smooth Fox Terrier, Ch.Oxonian, which she painted in 1905, forms part of the collection. It was once a popular practice to cross-breed the two coats and Oxonian is the result of such breeding.

Although Smooths predominate in the collection, there are two paintings of Wires. The first is a portrait by Arthur Wardle and could well be 'the picture of Ch.Cackler of Notts' as mentioned in the Duchess of Newcastle's bequest, although the dog's facial markings are not as pronounced as in other paintings of the dog. Cackler was the Duchess' first Wire Fox Terrier champion and there are those who consider him as the ancestor of every show Wire this century. Some judges considered him as being too big.

The second painting is a study by Nevison Arthur Loraine (fl.from 1889) of Ch.Kemphurst Superb. Loraine lived first in London and from 1908 at Esher in Surrey. He exhibited work at a number of galleries, including eight at the Royal Academy. Kemphurst Superb, who was originally registered as Crackley Superb, was born in 1926, bred by Bob Barlow, often described as probably the most successful terrier man who ever lived, and owned by George Howlett, one-time chairman of the General Committee of the Kennel Club. Her sire was Ch.Barry Benedict and she was the great-great-granddaughter of Comedian of Notts who traced back to Cackler of Notts. She was one of the top winning Wires who in 1927 won five best in show awards at championship shows, including the Kennel Club's own show.

'The Open Door' which was painted by Briton Riviere RA (1840-1920) in 1916 is considered by some to be the best picture in the collection (Plate 27). Certainly Riviere is one of the artists represented in the collection whose work is the best known to the wider public outside dogdom. Riviere was a member of a large Huguenot family of watchmakers, silversmiths, goldsmiths and artists who first

Plate 27
Briton Riviere, RA
(1840-1920).
'The Open Door'.
Signed with mongram
and dated 1916,
oil on canvas, 40" x 47".
Some consider this picture
as being the best in the
Kennel Club's collection.

settled in England in the 17th century. He was primarily an animal painter who at one time shared a studio with Heywood Hardy. He exhibited his work extensively and was elected a Royal Academician in 1881. He was a gentle man who loved animals and was fanatical about dogs. Like so many artists of his era he worked frequently in London Zoo.

His wife was obsessive about health and when Briton was asked to become President of the Royal Academy, she was adamant that he should not accept for it might be too much for his health, even though he never suffered illness. Riviere's painting of Sir R.W. Buchanan Jardine's Greyhound, Long Span, is a sentimental picture showing the dog in quiet, reflective mood, a mood that was perhaps more in keeping with the artist who was approaching the end of his life, rather than that of the victor of many a coursing meeting. In very unfavourable weather, Long Span won the Waterloo Cup in 1907 beating Glenbridge in the finals and it was the first Scottish victory since 1880. In 1908 he reached the semi-finals and ran again in 1909 and although beaten, he

won the Plate. Riviere's painting was presented to the Kennel Club by Francis Pickett, author of 'The Book of the Alsatian' and personal friend of the late Sir Malcolm Campbell, one time holder of the world land speed record.

Although in theory women had little control where important policy decisions were concerned, in reality a few were exceedingly good puppeteers. Women like Lorna, Countess Howe and Mrs. Florence Nagle managed to carry a lot of weight, Countess Howe in particular where field trials were concerned. It was Mrs.Nagle who challenged both the Jockey Club and the Kennel Club over their respective policies towards women. Women trainers and women members of the Kennel Club have much to thank her for.

The painting by Reuben Ward Binks (1880-1950) of seven of Countess Howe's black Labradors (Plate 28) is evidence of just how successful she was in the breed. The dogs shown are Ch.Barrie of Faircote, Ch.Gateley Ben, Ch. and FT Ch.Banchory Bolo, Ch.Banchory Bruco, Ch.Banchory Lucky, Ch.Banchory Sunspeck and Ch.Banchory Betsy. Countess

Plate 28
Reuben Ward Binks
(1880-1950).
Lorna, Countess Howe's
Labradors.
Signed and dated 1923,
gouache, 14" x 19".
The dogs are l. to r.
Ch.Barrie of Faircote,
Ch.Gateley Ben,
Ch.& F.T.Ch.Banchory
Bolo, Ch.Banchory
Bruco (back),
Ch.Banchory Lucky
(centre), Ch.Banchory
Sunspeck (front) and
Ch.Banchory Betsy.

Plate 29
Reuben Ward Binks
(1880-1950).
Mrs. Cottingham's
Golden Retriever,
Ch.Diver of Woolley.
Signed and dated 1928,
gouache, 10" x 13¹/₂".
All the Woolley champions
were painted by Binks.

Howe's (or Mrs.Quentin Dick as she then was) first Labrador was a dog called Scandal of Glynn, a grandson of Munden Sovereign who was owned by Lord Knutsford, once described by Countess Howe as "the breed's greatest benefactor." Scandal only sired one litter and when he died in 1917 his owner was keen to replace him with something which had his character; she had other dogs by this time but nothing which matched Scandal. It was her husband who managed to track down the only dog in Scandal's litter, who by this time had been through many hands. Banchory Bolo (as he was to be named), arrived at her London home in Grosvenor Crescent one February morning in 1918, a surly, heavily muzzled dog. With care and understanding she brought back his true Labrador character and he became a very influential dog, a champion in the field and on the bench and the breed's first dual champion. When he died in 1927 it was ten years before she could bring herself to have another personal dog. Lorna, Countess Howe who died in 1961 was the daughter of Major Ernest Charles Penn Curzon and her second marriage was as the third wife of the 4th Earl, Richard George Penn GCVO, 6th Viscount Curzon.

Ward Binks is remembered best for his paintings of gundogs and a recent acquisition hanging in the Kennel Club is his study of the Golden Retriever, Ch.Diver of Woolley *(Plate 29)*. His owner, Mrs.Cottingham, had one of the strongest and largest kennels in the breed during the '20s and '30s. All the Woolley champions were painted by Ward Binks.

Binks worked in gouache and his style is very distinctive. He was born in Bolton but spent much of his life in the Lake District. He was considered throughout his life a great eccentric and both he and his wife became Christian Scientists and some thought his death was perhaps premature. It was believed that the habit throughout his life of continually licking the end of his paint brush did little to help his health. Artistically there are other dog artists who would undoubtedly be considered more competent than Binks but few gathered around them the patrons which he did. Apart from Countess Howe and Mrs.Cottingham, there were King George V and other members of the Royal Family, the Duke of Hamilton, Dr.Turton Price, the du Ponts and Mrs.Rockefeller Dodge in America and the Maharajah Dhiraj of Patiala in India. On one visit to India alone Binks spent eight months just painting the Maharajah's gundogs. The Maharajah of Patiala was given a Maybach Zeppelin car by Adolf Hitler in hope of support should war break out and this was recently sold in Geneva for £213,000.

Mrs.Nagle was the daughter of Sir (William) George Watson 1st Baronet, chairman of the Maypole Dairy Co.Ltd. until he retired in 1924 and an advocate of the system of copartnership. On her death in 1988 aged 94, the Kennel Club acquired two large pastels by Cecil Charles Windsor Aldin (1870-1935) of two of Mrs.Nagle's Irish Setters. Mrs.Nagle was a great friend of Aldin, the friendship being formed through Mrs.Nagle's friendship at finishing school in Paris with Aldin's daughter, Gwen, and it was Aldin who was instrumental in obtaining Mrs.Nagle her first Irish Wolfhound, the breed for which she will forever be remembered in the show ring.

Aldin is one of the best known of the 20th century sporting artists and illustrators who had studied art under Albert Moore in Kensington, the National Art Training School and at Frank Calderon's School of Animal Painting. Aldin organised the first gymkhana for children in 1927. The two Irish Setters featured are FT Ch.Sulhampstead Valla D'Or *(Plate 30)* and FT Ch.Sulhampstead Sheilin D'Or *(Plate 31)*. Mrs.Nagle kept the Sulhampstead flag flying at field trials from the twenties to the sixties, only giving up when her handler, George Abbott, retired. She had 18 field trial champions, an enviable record. She held strong beliefs that her dogs should be good lookers as well as good workers and her first Irish Setter, Ben D'Or, was a challenge certificate winner on the bench as well as being placed in trials.

Sheilin was born in 1925 and Valla in 1926 and both were also winners on the show bench. Sheilin was the first Irish Setter to win the Champion Stakes doing so in 1927 and again in 1930. Her owner rated her as her best ever Setter. Mrs.Nagle, a Vice President of the Kennel Club, maintained that Sheilin and Valla were inseparable in life and should remain so in death and their pictures hang side by side. A model in silver of Sheilin mounted on a plinth was presented by Mrs.Nagle to the English Setter Club for the best Irish Setter at the Spring Trial Meeting.

White metal linked collar, the alternate links with floral embossed decoration, 22" long. The centre plaque is engraved 'Cato Manchester Show. First prize 1861. First prize 1862'.

"Ch. Loga of the Arctic"

Plate 32
Frederick Thomas Daws (b.1878).
Miss Marion Keyte Perry's
Samoyed, Ch.Loga of the Arctic.
Signed and dated 1932,
oil on canvas, 22" x 16".
Loga was his owner's constant
companion.

Two other large Aldin pastels hang in the collection. The first shows the Deerhound, Brutus of Bridge Sollers, a dog owned by Miss Linton whose Geltsdale kennel became a major force in the breed. Brutus was born in 1925 and was a gift to Agnes Linton from her father and it is reputed that he commissioned Aldin to paint Brutus' picture. It was bequeathed by Miss Linton to Miss Nora Hartley of the Rotherwood Deerhounds who in turn bequeathed it to the Kennel Club.

While Brutus is shown in reflective mood, the other Aldin, the German Shepherd Dog Dick Turpin, shows a dog full of anticipation, perhaps of life ahead. Aldin painted this picture

for a groom to give his bride as a wedding present, Dick Turpin being her pet.

Miss Marion Keyte Perry was chairman of the Ladies' branch of the Kennel Club from 1948-1963 and through her involvement with the club it is home to one of Frederick T.Daws' better paintings of a dog, namely her Samoyed Ch.Loga of the Arctic *(Plate 32)*. Daws was born in 1878 and exhibited work at the Royal Academy and other galleries and although he is best known as a painter, he was probably artistically more accomplished as a sculptor. He executed a number of fine bronzes and for Royal Doulton he modelled most of the dogs in their Champion Dogs series. He modelled the

31

large English Setter with a pheasant, first issued by Doulton in 1941, one of which is in the collection.

Loga was born in 1925 and bred by Mrs.D.Edwards whose stock, according to Miss Keyte Perry, "raised the whole standard of the breed." Loga won six CCs in all, became a famous stud dog and his owner's constant companion.

Another Daws in the collection is a recent acquisition being bought at Christie's Sporting Art and Dogs sale in July 1998. This shows the Bulldog, Ch.Tintagel *(Plate 33)*, standing four-square . Tintagel was owned and bred by Mrs.Surtees Monkland, was born in 1916 and was one of a number of famous champion Bulldogs owned by Mrs.Monkland. A similar study of a Bulldog is one of an unnamed dog by Arthur Wardle.

Two Airedale paintings hang in the collection, both showing dogs in the characteristic show pose for the breed. Painted some 20 years apart, they emphasise just how little many of the long-legged terrier breeds have changed compared with some of the shorter-legged breeds. The earlier of the two was painted by Arthur Wardle *(Plate 34)*, being the original for the print,

'Airedales of the 20th Century'. This was first published by Mansell & Co. of Holloway, London, who did much to raise the standard of dog prints and make a wider public aware of the quality of British dogs. He went broke during the first World War and sold his plates to Spratts who, in their turn, sold many on. Some of the prints originally published by Mansell are still being published today by Ross, including the Airedales and the Totteridge XI. Mansell was a great supporter of the Kennel Club and the collection includes a few prints specially inscribed by Mansell to the Kennel Club.

The dogs featured are Holland Buckley's Ch.Mistress Royal and Ch.Master Royal. Mistress Royal was by Ch.Master Blair who was a son of Briar Test, about whom it has been said was responsible more than any other dog for the Airedale as we see it today. Mistress Royal, who was considered by her owner "a most remarkable bitch", was out of Claverhouse Enchantress, who played a tremendous part at that time in the future history of the breed. Her sire was Ch.Clonmel Monarch, who was sold to America by Holland Buckley for what was considered at the time the largest sum ever given for a Terrier.

Plate 34
Arthur Wardle
(1864-1949).
Holland Buckley's
Airedale Terriers,
Ch.Mistress Royal and
Ch.Master Royal.
Signed and dated 1904,
oil on canvas, 21" x 27".
Both dogs descended
from the famous
Ch.Clonmel Monarch.
Reproduced with
permission of The
Thomas Ross Collection.

Plate 35
Frances L. Fairman (1836-1923).
The Chow, Ch.Chow VIII.
Signed and dated 1899,
oil on canvas, 14" x 12".
This dog was the first champion
in the breed and passed through
many hands.

Large leather collar 30" long with brass
fittings. The brass plaque is engraved
'Mr Alex' Cookes Dog of y' Grainge in
Coggeshall. Anno 1729'. The collar
was found by Mr. Herbert Goode in a
Coggeshall curiosity shop and acquired
from him by E. W. Jaquet. It was
presented to The Kennel Club by G. D.
Howlett, Esq. in 1922.

Mistress Royal was bred by Mrs.M.Cuthell and Master Royal was bred by Holland Buckley in partnership with Royston Mills from an unregistered Clonmel bitch by Clonmel Chiperic, whose sire was Monarch.

The later of the two Airedale pictures is by F.T.Daws and shows Mr.H.Keighley's Ch.Brewers Dictator who was painted in 1922 when the dog was just 12 months old and at the start of a highly successful show career which included the dog CC at Crufts in 1923.

Perhaps more so than any artist, Frances L.Fairman (1836-1923) is associated with the oriental breeds and in particular the Japanese Chin. She was involved in the dog world, being very active in the Ladies' Kennel Association and had many lady dog breeders as her patrons, including Queen Alexandra, herself a Japanese Chin fancier.

The headstudy of the Chow, Ch.Chow VIII, is typical of Fairman's soft impressionistic style (Plate 35). The dog was born in 1890 and became the first champion in the breed and was winning prizes at Crufts until 1900. Chow passed through many hands during his long show career, one theory being his poor temperament to the extent that at times he could not be handled. The painting was given

to the Kennel Club by the late Owen Grindey, one time secretary of the two Birmingham shows and himself a Chow enthusiast.

Another Fairman in the collection is a particularly fine study of a Schipperke and two puppies playing in straw in a yard (Plate 36). It is a fine example of the type of Schipperke which was developing in England at the time. The dog is Ch.Yaap who was born in 1897, ten years after the first Schipperkes came in to this country. Yaap was by El Dorado out of Ch.Satanita and was the eighth male champion in the breed, his mother, who was also by El Dorado, being the third female champion. El Dorado sired a total of seven champion children. Yaap was bred by Mrs.Heard, a successful breeder of Schipperkes, and was owned by Mrs.Skewes-Cox, whose son, Major T.Skewes-Cox, presented the painting to the Kennel Club in 1948. The two puppies in the picture may be two of Yaap's children, or merely added to give dimension to the composition.

Another painting in the collection featuring a first champion shows the Schnauzer, Ch.Cranbourne Lupin (Plate 37). She was painted by the equestrian artist, H.Harris (op.c.1910-1946). Lupin was born in 1929, bred by Captain and Mrs.Hornyold and was by Bodo von der Ludwigshohe ex Otti von der

Plate 37
H. Harris
(op.c.1910-1946).
Captain Leslie Williams
Schnauzer,
Ch.Cranbourne Lupin.
Signed, oil on canvas,
16" x 20".
This bitch was the first
British champion in the
breed.

Plate 38
Paul Mahler, French,
(op.late 19th/early 20th
century). Two Irish Setters
in a landscape. Signed,
watercolour,
9" x 12".
This is a rare example of
Mahler's original work in
colour.

Ludwigshohe. She was owned by Captain Leslie Williams and had a successful show career winning 11 CCs, including four at Crufts. Williams was interested in the working side of the breed just as much as the show ring and two other paintings of his dogs in the collection, both by Harris, feature Brenda of Ashways and Titus of Ashways, both successful in Working Trials.

Few pieces in the collection are by artists from overseas. One exception is a watercolour of two Irish Setters *(Plate 38)* by the French animal artist and illustrator, Paul Mahler (op.late 19th/early 20th century). Although he had work exhibited at the Paris Salon in 1897, he will never rank alongside the great dog artists. To the understanding of the evolution of breeds, though, he is an important artist. He was commissioned to record every breed of dog and nearly all these works were published in the *Journal 'L' Acclimatation.* Much of his work also appeared in Comte Henry de Byland's *Dogs of all Nations* and other dog books which have followed. At least 90 of his illustrations were published in postcard form. It is Mahler's work, much of which is of named dogs, which has to

a great extent dictated the way we understand visually today how many breeds were at the turn of the century, particularly many of the continental breeds which have become so popular. Of necessity much of Mahler's work was in black and white, the Setters are a rare example of his colour work.

Lilian Cheviot (op.c.1894-1920's) was yet another artist who studied at Frank Calderon's School. She established her reputation as an animal and equestrian painter and counted the Earl of Lonsdale among her patrons. Several of her equestrian paintings were auctioned at Lowther Castle sale in 1947. Hanging in the Kennel Club is a study of the Pekingese, Ch.Chu-Erh of Alderbourne *(Plate 39)*, the first of a long line of Pekingese champions for Mrs.Ashton Cross and her daughters. Chu-Erh was born in 1905 and bred by Mrs.Weaver whose doctor had advised her to take up Pekingese breeding as she needed to take life more easily.

Mrs.Ashton Cross bought Chu-Erh at three months of age for the then unheard of price of £150. It is said that her husband almost

Plate 40
Margaret Collyer
(op.c.1897-1915).
Black Spaniel of the sort
of Cocker being bred by
C. A. Phillips and
Mrs. Fytche.
Signed and dated 1914,
oil on canvas, 20" x 24".

Plate 41
Marion Roger Hamilton
Harvey (b.1886).
Mrs. Veronica Collins
Dachshunds, Ch.Firs
Redline and Ch.Firs Red
Letter of Kelvindale.
Signed, pastel,
17$^1/_2$ x 23$^1/_2$".
Mrs. Collins was one of
the few Dachshund
breeders who managed to
continue breeding during
the last war.

Plate 42
Andie (Andie Pasinger),
American, (contemporary).
Miss Veronica Tudor Williams
Basenji, Fula of the Congo.
Signed and dated 1975,
varnished pastel, 20" x 16".
Fula was born in the
South Sudan in 1959.
Photograph: Prudence
Cuming Associates Limited.

collapsed when he heard what she had paid. Chu-Erh proved a good investment, for not only did he become a big winner in the breed, including winning the CC at Crufts in both 1907 and '08, but he was the foundation of a kennel which virtually dominated the breed for the first three quarters of this century and is behind most Pekingese today. It is reputed that Mrs.Ashton Cross refused £32,000 for the dog to go to America.

Margaret Collyer (op.c.1897-1915) was another woman artist working around the same time as Lilian Cheviot and who also established her reputation as an animal and equestrian painter. The painting of the black Spaniel in the collection which Collyer completed in 1914 is a particularly fine example of dog portraiture of the period *(Plate 40)*. It also stands as a fine example of how type in breeds was being established at the time, for this dog shows certain Field and Cocker characteristics. It is probably the artist's idea of an ideal Cocker Spaniel of the period, but is the sort of Cocker

that could have come from either the Rivington kennel of C.A.Phillips, or the Fulmer kennel of Mrs.Fytche.

Both the dog and horse worlds have provided comfortable livings for many artists, one of whom was the Scottish born artist, Marion Roger Hamilton Harvey (b.1886). Harvey worked mainly in pastels and crayons and the study of two red Dachshunds in the collection is typical of the artist's work *(Plate 41)*. The dogs were owned by Veronica Collins who was chairman of the Dachshund Club of Scotland for 50 years and served on the Scottish Kennel Club Executive for 25 years. She was also one of few Dachshund breeders who managed to continue breeding during the Second World War. The dogs are Ch.Firs Redline and his daughter, Ch.Red Letter of Kelvindale. Redline was sired by one of Mrs.Huggins' great winners, Ch.Firs Black Velvet, and on both sides he went back to another great dog and sire in the breed, Mme.P.P.Rikovsky's German import, Int.Ch.Wolf vom Birkenschloss.

Plate 43
William Tymym, MBE
(1902-1990).
Rottweillers.
Signed and dated 1976,
coloured chalks,
32" x 45".
This painting decorated
the British Rottweiller
Association's stand at
Crufts in 1976.
Reproduced courtesy the
Oxford Partnership.

Four minor paintings in the collection help to illustrate its diversity. The first is a headstudy of a Bedlington Terrier by W.H.Durham (op.from c.1890). The second features the Scottish Terrier, Mrs.F.T.K.Woodworth's Piper of Penroath, a winner in the ring but one of three Scotties owned by Mrs.Woodworth who starred in Rudyard Kipling's *His Apologies*. Piper was painted by S.Ripley (op.1930s-'40s). The third was painted by Harry Glover who wrote and illustrated *Toydogs* which was published in 1977 but who is remembered more as a judge of dogs rather than an artist. It features two white Bull Terriers and a Yorkshire Terrier beside an old cold frame with a dead rat at their feet. One suspects by the dogs' pristine condition, they had little to do with the fate of the rat.

The fourth is a headstudy of the Basenji, Fula of the Congo *(Plate 42)*. Two plaques on the picture's frame tell the story of the painting, it being presented to Veronica Tudor Williams at Seattle, Washington 'In Memory of Fula' by the Evergreen Basenji Club. Fula's portrait is inscribed 'Fula of the Congo 1959-1974' and signed Andie (Andie Pasinger) and dated 1975.

Fula was an extraordinary dog. She was born in the South Sudan in 1959 and bought by Miss Tudor Williams on one of her journeys to Africa for 35 shillings. She was at the time of

her purchase thought to be about ten weeks old and was wearing a tiny collar of bright coloured cotton tied in a bow and according to Miss Tudor Williams "she looked adorable." Like all the native dogs she was covered in fleas.

She was never shown because Lady Nutting, then Basenji Club president, was adamant that with her primitive and isolated background, she would have little, if any, immunity to English germs. She did, though, establish herself in Basenji history in this country as an outstanding brood. Writing in *The Daily Express* in 1968, Stanley Dangerfield had this to say: "Although imported only nine short years ago, all the world's top Basenjis are now descended from Fula. No dog of any breed has ever made a more dramatic contribution to progress."

Before moving on one should perhaps mention the pastel signed and dated 1968 of three Cairn Terriers heads by Marjorie Cox. Miss Cox is perhaps the most prolific of the post Second World War artists and works very much in the manner of the early 'primitive' jobbing artists. A non-driver, she waits until she has a quantity of commissions in a given area and then takes the train to a central point. Once there she is transported around by her clients from one to another.

Jessica Holm
(Contemporary).
'Lady Lush. The Pointer,
Ghillie, enjoying a
summer afternoon in an
English country garden.
Signed with initials
and dated 1997.
Pencil, 15" x 15".
Reproduced courtesy Jessica
Holm

The collection is fortunate in housing a painting by one of this country's most highly regarded post war artists, William Timym MBE (1902-1990). This is a large coloured chalk study of two Rottweilers *(Plate 43)*. It was completed by Timym to decorate the British Rottweiler Association's stand at Crufts in 1976 when held at Olympia, the second year breed stands were a feature of the show. The then secretary, Joan Adams, and her husband were friends of Timym and he offered the picture which is an amalgam of dogs. When Kenneth Adams became a member of the Kennel Club in 1977, he and Joan presented it to the Club.

Timym was Austrian by birth and grew up in Vienna and studied at the Vienna Academy of Art. He had several exhibitions of his work in Vienna and Cologne before he left Austria in 1938 due to Nazi occupation. He moved to England where his reputation, primarily as a sculptor, soon became established. He had a long standing association with London Zoo and sculpted a life-size bronze of a lion's head, Guy the gorilla and Chi-Chi the giant panda. He also did portrait commissions including Sir Bertrand Russell, Sir Malcolm Sargent and Sir Francis Chichester. A whole generation of

people will be familiar with Bengo the Boxer puppy on T.V., another of Timym's creations.

The collection also houses a number of important photographic portraits, human as well as canine. By the closing years of the 19th century, photography had developed into an art form in its own right and the large framed photograph of Dr.J.H.Salter *(Plate 44)*, a member of the Committee of the Kennel Club, is an outstanding example of photographic portraiture. Salter began keeping dogs in 1858 and like de Trafford was a person who helped establish Britain as an important producer of livestock. He was interested in coursing, field trials and the show ring.

During his time in dogs he owned over 1,000 Greyhounds, 300 Retrievers, including many important Curlies, 250 Pointers, about the same number of Sussex Spaniels, nearly 200 English Setters, about 150 Field Spaniels, over 100 Irish Setters, 50 Cocker Spaniels, a dozen Clumbers and nearly 100 Fox Terriers.

The photograph shows the doctor in the guise of field trial judge. A newspaper report in 1909 of a field trial judged by Salter noted the extraordinary feat he had achieved. He had

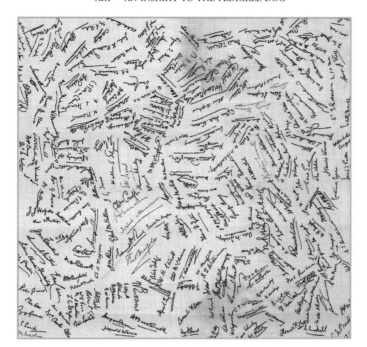

Plate 45
A silk cloth with some 200
reproduced autograph
signatures sold to raise funds
for Manchester Dogs' Home.
1910, 32" x 32".

arrived in his motor car having driven the journey of over 50 miles from his home in a little under three hours! Salter was the seconder to Redmond's proposal to found a Ladies Branch of the Kennel Club.

One of the more unusual pieces in the collection is a cloth embroidered in silk in 1910 with some 200 autograph signatures of some of the most noted exhibitors and others interested in dogs *(Plate 45)*. The cloth was the idea of the Misses Preston of Rusholme, Manchester, to raise funds for Manchester Dogs' Home.

Reproductions were sold at a charge of 2s.6d and were obtainable from the Misses Preston.

To see how many names one can recognise in a given time is the sort of after dinner game doggy historians could play - it also becomes addictive by just trying to recognise one more name. It is a veritable Who's Who and for my part I soon found Maud Earl, Francis Redmond, W.McClandish, Harold Warnes, F.M.Jowett, Aubrey Ireland (at one time my doctor), Theo Marples, E.W.Jaquet, Walter Glyn, Arthur J.Marples, J.B.Jelly Dudley, Charles Cruft, Countess of Aberdeen, Kathleen Pilkington, Holland Buckley, Minna Allen, Lady Betty, Henry St.John Cooper, James Farrow and Lilla Ives. Others, I am sure, would instantly come up with another list of 20.

Collection built on bequests and gifts

The bulk of the Kennel Club's collection of art has been built up by bequest, gift, or donation. Within recent years a buying policy has been introduced to extend the collection through the purchase of historical pieces or to add an artist or breed not already represented in the collection. The extension, though, of any such collection is always going to be largely dependent upon bequests and gifts and bequeathing a private collection to such as the Kennel Club does ensure that it stays together and will be housed where it is appreciated.

One such collection which is bequeathed to come to the Kennel Club will, for example, introduce both a breed and an artist not at

present in the collection. The picture is an unusual composition for the artist and shows a group of sled dogs, *(Plate 46)* the artist being George Vernon Stokes (1873-1954). Stokes was born in London and educated privately, his work was exhibited at the Royal Academy and other galleries and for a while he worked in Carlisle. The museum there has a collection of his work. He is perhaps best remembered today for his illustrative work, and he was also the author of *The Drawing and Painting of Dogs* which was published in 1934.

The Kennel Club houses some important trophies owned by individual clubs and which are no longer competed for. Their value is such

41

Plate 46
George Vernon Stokes
(1873-1954).
A group of sled dogs.
Signed, oil on canvas,
18" x 24".
An unusual composition
for the artist.

that the clubs feel they should be in a safe place and where they can be seen. There are three outstanding examples worthy of note.

First is 'The Presidents 100 Guinea Challenge Cup' *(Plate 47)* owned by the Setter and Pointer Club and now valued at £18,000. This silver trophy was presented by Professor L. Turton Price, a surgeon in Edinburgh, owner of the famous Crombie gundog kennel. Standing some 32" high, including the plinth, it is hallmarked for 1926 and was made by James Dixon & Sons, manufacturers of a large variety of silver items. It was won first in 1926 by Turton Price's O By Jingo, winner of 13 C.Cs., a dominant influence as a stud and the first English Setter to go best in show at an all breeds championship show in this country.

The second trophy is another gundog trophy and is owned by The English Setter Club. It is a brace trophy, such stakes no longer existing. Called 'The Pure Type Challenge Trophy For Braces', *(Plate 48)* it shows two very finely modelled dogs in silver - a Pointer and a Setter - on a naturalistic base, and they stand on a

plinth carrying the winners' names. It was on offer first in 1896 at the autumn trials of the International Pointer and Setter Society and was won by Sir W.W. Wynn's Pointers, Rob O'Cymru and Ben O'Cymru. It was won outright by B.J. Warwick, whose most famous dog was possibly F.T.Ch.Compton Trim, winner of the International Pointer and Setter Society's International Champion Stake in 1912. Warwick presented it to the English Setter Club. Hallmarked for 1896, it was made by the Goldsmiths and Silversmiths Company, Regent Street, London and stands some 18½" high.

The third trophy is a bronze model of a cropped Great Dane standing on a base, the whole 16" high. Known as 'The Great Dane Challenge Trophy for Best Dog', *(Plate 49)* it is owned by The Great Dane Club and was presented to the Kennel Club by Mrs. Horsfall who imported two Great Danes from Germany in 1896. It was won first by Mrs. Horsfall's Ch. Hannibal of Redgrave, one of her two imports and one of the top winning Great Danes of the 19th century. Mrs. Horsfall won

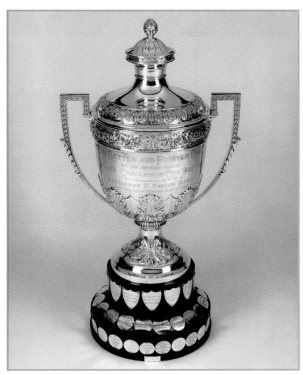

Plate 47 'The Presidents 100 Guinea Challenge Cup'. Hallmarked for 1926 and made by James Dixon & Sons. 32" high, including plinth. (Reproduced courtesy The Setter and Pointer Club).

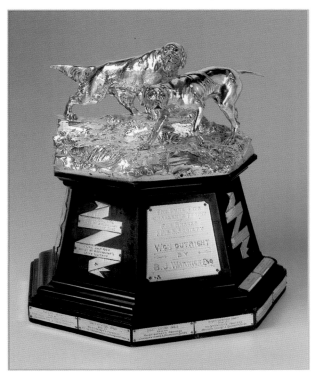

Plate 48 R. H. Moore, Sculpt. (op.c.1868-c.1910). 'The Pure Type Challenge Trophy For Braces'. Two finely modelled dogs on a naturalistic base. Hallmarked for 1896 and made by the Goldsmiths and Silversmiths Company. 18¹/₂" high. (Reproduced courtesy The English Setter Club).

Plate 49 R. H. Moore, Sculpt. (op.c.1868-c.1910). 'The Great Dane Challenge Trophy for Best Dog'. Bronze model of a cropped Great Dane on a base, the whole 16" high. (Reproduced courtesy The Great Dane Club).

Plate 50 'The Keddell Memorial Trophy for Best in Show at Crufts'. Standing some 34" high, including base, and weighing 300 ounces, it is hallmarked for 1925 and was made by Martin Hall & Co.

43

the trophy every time it was on offer up to 1907 with five different dogs.

The Pointer and Setter and the Great Dane were sculpted by R.H.Moore (op.c.1868-c.1910).

The Kennel Club owns some very important trophies in its own right of which the Keddell Memorial Trophy, now awarded for Best in Show at Crufts, *(Plate 50)* is perhaps the best known and most photographed dog show trophy in the world. It is, though, not a memorial to a great dog breeder, or a famous dog but to Robert Keddell, show manager at Charles Cruft's show from 1894 until 1924. Standing some two feet high, weighing 300 ounces and made by Martin Hall & Co., makers of a large variety of wares, this two handled decorated silver cup and cover, which today can never be held by the winner, was first awarded in 1925, valued then at a mere £125. Originally a breed trophy, it was 'open to all for the best of one breed, the breed to be different each year.'

The first breed to receive the trophy was the 'Alsatian Wolf Dog' and the first winner was Francis Pickett's German-bred Ch.Caro of Welham. It was last awarded as a breed trophy in 1937 and won on that occasion by Joe Braddon's Irish Setter, Ch.Wendover Biddy. For the last two shows run by the Cruft family it was awarded for Best in Show, being won on both occasions by H.S.Lloyd's Cocker Exquisite Model of Ware.

During the war years the Kennel Club bought Crufts show from Charles Cruft's widow for a sum which Cruft's personal secretary, Miss Hardingham, considered was far too low. She herself would have liked the opportunity to have bought the show but Mrs.Cruft preferred it to go to the Kennel Club, an organisation Cruft had considered as being his great rival and whose shows he rarely attended, preferring to send his secretaries who would then report back.

After the war the Kennel Club dropped their own prestigious Kennel Club Show in favour of the better known and more flamboyantly run Crufts Show. At the first Crufts Show run by the Kennel Club in 1948, the Keddell Memorial Trophy was once again offered for Best in Show and, with the exception of the years 1969 to 1972, when it was demoted to the Reserve Best Terrier Trophy, has remained the major trophy.

For the years 1969 to 1972 the Best in Show trophy was the Daytona Beach Trophy *(Plate 51)* which had been offered alongside the Keddell from 1952 to 1968. Made by Tiffany and Co. in America and equally impressive, although less ornate than the Keddell, the trophy had been presented to Sir Malcolm Campbell by the Vice President of America, Charles G.Dawes, on behalf of the City of Daytona Beach. The trophy commemorated Campbell winning the International Speed Trials in February 1928 with a then world record speed of 206.956 mph.

In 1951 Campbell's widow, Lady Dorothea Campbell, who owned and exhibited Miniature Poodles and who had been divorced from Campbell since 1940, presented the trophy to the Kennel Club for Best in Show at Crufts. The reason for the presentation is not known for certain, although in 'Who Was Who', Sir Malcolm's interests included 'dog breeding, Alsatians and Airedale Terriers'. It could be that 'Alsatian' breeder and personal friend of Campbell, Francis Pickett, had something to do with the presentation, for he presented to the Kennel Club Riviere's painting of the Greyhound, Long Span.

The Lakeland Terrier, Ch.Stingray of Derryabah, won Best in Show at Crufts in 1967, having won the Terrier Group the year before. He was sired by one of the greatest Lakelands of all time, Ch.Hensington Carefree, owned and bred by Mr. & Mrs.Wilf Postlethwaite and handled, as was Carefree, by Albert Langley. After his Crufts win, Stingray was exported to the United States, where he won Best in Show at Westminster in 1968, the only dog of any breed to top both Crufts and Westminster. The trophy made by Tiffany in the form of a silver bowl *(Plate 52)*, which was awarded to Stingray when he won Westminster, was presented to Crufts Dog Show by the Westminster Kennel Club on the occasion of Crufts centenary show in January 1991.

Engraved on the trophy is the famous Westminster Pointer, equally as famous as the Crufts St.Bernard. As Crufts is associated with one man, so to an extent is Westminster, it taking its name from the Westminster Breeding Kennel, whose co-founder was Alexander Stewart Webb and who became the first President of Westminster Show. Webb had been a Civil War general who played a crucial role in turning the tide for the Union soldiers at the

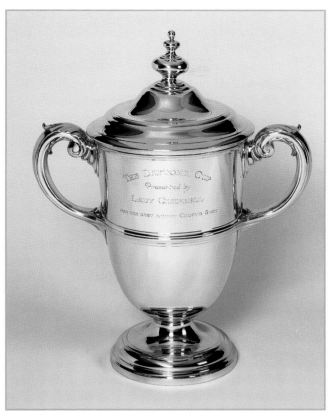

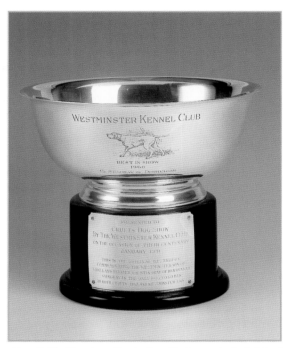

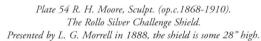

Plate 52 The Westminster Best in Show Trophy won by the Lakeland Terrier, Ch.Stingray of Derryabah, in 1968. The silver bowl was made by Tiffany & Co. and stands 11$\frac{1}{2}$" high. It was presented to Crufts Dog Show by the Westminster Kennel Club in 1991.

Plate 51 Daytona Beach Trophy made by Tiffany & Co. in America. Presented to The Kennel Club by Lady Dorothea Campbell in 1951. 26" high.

Plate 54 R. H. Moore, Sculpt. (op.c.1868-1910). The Rollo Silver Challenge Shield. Presented by L. G. Morrell in 1888, the shield is some 28" high.

Plate 53 One of the original five Send Gold Vases given to The Kennel Club in 1930 by Gordon Stewart for the Best of Each Group at the old Kennel Club Shows. They were made by the Goldsmiths and Silversmiths Co. and stand 17" high.

45

Battle of Gettysburg. The Westminster Breeding Kennel was noted for its fine Pointers and the Pointer used as the show's logo depicts a dog called Sensation (late Don), who was bred in England by J.D.Humphries of Shrewsbury in 1874 and became the Westminster Breeding Kennel's most active stud dog.

The best known trophies from the old Kennel Club Shows are the Send Gold Vases *(Plate 53)*, five of which were given to the Kennel Club in 1930 by Gordon Stewart and were offered for the Best of Each Group - Sporting (Hound), Gundog, Terrier, Toy and Non Sporting (Working and Utility). The latter was won for the first time by Stewart himself with the Great Dane, Ch.Mavis of Send.

Each vase is made of 9ct gold and stands some 17" high and in 1930 were each valued at £162, a far cry from their many thousands today and, as with the Keddell, they can no longer be held by the winners. They were made by the Goldsmiths and Silversmiths Co., who became Garrard & Co.Ltd., the Crown Jewellers. After the war these trophies were put in store until 1965 when they were once again offered for the best of each group and with the splitting of the Non-Sporting group into Working and Utility, a further gold vase was made. With the splitting of the Working group into Working and Pastoral in 1999, yet another vase was made, although sadly on this occasion in silver gilt.

Appropriately two Great Danes masks form the two handles to each vase and the finials for the covers represent a breed from each group Bloodhound, Cocker Spaniel, Airedale, Pekingese, Great Dane, Bulldog and Rough Collie.

Gordon Stewart's great rival in Danes was James Rank. Both were exceedingly wealthy men and although Stewart was passionate to the point of being fanatical about his dogs and imported many from Germany, he had no real interest in shows. He took up showing to prove that his dogs were equal to those of his rival Rank, for there was no love lost between the two men. Perhaps the Gold Vases were a form of one up man ship on the part of Stewart over Rank.

A trophy from the old Kennel Club shows and one which has not been awarded for years, is 'The Rollo Silver Challenge Shield' *(Plate 54)*. As with the Great Dane Club's Trophy and the

Two Rosenthal Italian Greyhounds/Whippets, the sitting one 6" high, the recumbent one 6¹/₂" long, the latter signed on the base T. Karner, one of the chief modellers of dogs at the factory. These models were the most popular sellers in the range and were withdrawn from production in the 1970's. They were part of a bequest to The Kennel Club from the late Mrs. Ann Argyle of the Harque Whippets.

English Setter Club's Trophy, the head of the Bloodhound in high relief within a garland was modelled by R.H.Moore. Moore was more adept as a sculptor than he was a painter. The collection houses one of his paintings in addition to the drawing of Joachim's Beagles. The oil is of an Irish Terrier from the days when the breed was cropped and shows an unnamed dog beside a dead rabbit. Moore is listed as an animal and sporting illustrator, sculptor and black and white artist and in the dog world he is perhaps best known for his pen and ink drawings for C.H.Lane's 'All About Dogs', published in 1900.

The Rollo Shield was competed for by Bloodhounds and was for the best dog or bitch in the Open Classes at the Kennel Club's winter and summer shows. Presented by L.G.Morrell in 1888, the shield is some 28" high and was originally valued at 50gns. The dog is probably Rollo who was bred by Mr.E.Reynold's Ray and owned by Major Bradford of Harrow. Rollo was born in 1873 and became a champion, he was sired by Ch.Roswell out of Ch.Peeress and was a typical example of Victorian inbreeding to establish type. Of his recorded great-great-grandparents, all but three are Rufus, Welcome, Druid and Dewlap.

The collection also houses a number of historically important models of dogs. The oldest of these would be the Borzoi, Ch.Tsaretsa, *(Plate 55)* which stands some 15¹/₂" high. Tradition has it that it was cast from melted-down trophies won by the hound and the ebonised base bears plaques proclaiming Tsaretsa's many wins. Hallmarked for 1900, the model was supplied by Dobson & Son of 32 Piccadilly, jewellers of some note and also suppliers of high quality silver and plated items.

By commissioning Dobsons to supply the model, the hound's owner, the Duchess of Newcastle, was in good company, as some years earlier Queen Victoria had from them a ewer which she presented for the winner of the Guernsey Race. Dobson's also supplied for an unnamed Eastern potentate, a silver tray and table measuring seven feet in diameter.

The Duchess of Newcastle was responsible in no small part for establishing the Borzoi in this country. Ch.Tsaretsa was one of her most successful hounds in the show ring as well as being a successful brood. She was one of those singled out for her type and stood 31¹/₂" high, with a 12 1/4" head length and a chest 36" in girth. Tsaretsa came from Gen.Boldariff in Russia, being by Pilai Podar out of Kolpitsa and was born on the 1st February, 1895.

Like Stewart, James Rank imported many Great Danes from Germany. One of the kennels in that country which was to the fore was Karl Farber's 'Saalburg' kennel, made famous by the great stud dog, Ch.Dolf von der Saalburg. Dolf's sire was Ch.Bosco von der Saalburg, whose blood became influential in the breed outside Germany. After a successful career in Germany, Bosco's daughter, Ch.Etta von der Saalburg, went to the States where she was equally successful in the ring and went on to produce eight champion children. She is still behind many of today's winning Danes in the States. Rank imported Etta's sister to this country, to which he added his 'Ouborough' prefix.

A bronze of Bosco is in the Kennel Club's art collection *(Plate 56)*. Sculpted by Ernst von Otto, a brilliant sculptor and author on German dogs (including *German Dogs in Words and Pictures,* published in English in 1928 and dedicated to 'His Highness the Maharaja Dhiraj of Patiala') the bronze stands some 14" high and shows the dog with characteristically cropped ears and although the dog was fawn, his model has a black patination. The base bears a plaque inscribed 'W.G.(Bill) Siggers 1896-1984'. Siggers had a long association with Rank's kennel, dogs in general and the Great Dane in particular and for many he will forever be 'Mr Great Dane'.

One of the larger pieces of sculpture in the collection is a bronze of the Deerhound, Ch.Prothetic of Ross *(Plate 57)*, which stands some 21" high and is mounted on a naturalistic base. It was sculpted by Louis Paul Jonas (1894-1971) and is dated 1938. It was presented to the Kennel Club by the hound's breeders, the Misses Loughrey who lived in Londonderry. Jonas was an Hungarian who emigrated to America at the age of 14. His work includes a monumental sculpture of a bear and her cub in the City Park in Denver, which is somewhat poignantly called 'Grizzly's Last Stand'.

The sisters were two of the most successful and influential breeders of Deerhounds and Prothetic, who was by Pharic of Ross ex Ch.Aesthetic of Ross, was born in 1932, and one of their more successful hounds. The Misses

Plate 55
The Borzoi, Ch.Tsaretsa, one of the Duchess of Newcastle's successful hounds. Hallmarked for 1900, the silver model was supplied by Dobson & Son, Piccadilly and stands 15 1/2".

Plate 56
Ernst von Otto, German, Sculpt. (first half of 20th century). Bronze model of Karl Faber's Great Dane, Ch.Bosco von der Saalburg. 14" high.

Plate 57
Louis Paul Jonas, American, Sculpt, (1894-1971). Bronze model of the Misses Loughrey's Deerhound, Ch.Prothetic of Ross. 21" high.

*Plate 59 Doris Lindner, Sculpt. (1896-1979). Bronze model of
Mr. & Mrs. Wilson Wileys' Boxer, Ch. Wardrobes Miss Mink. 9" high.
Many consider Miss Mink to have been the best Boxer ever bred.*

Loughrey were two very strong characters and when the border went up in Ireland, like some other Anglo Irish ladies of the time, they flatly refused to be stopped and interrogated. It was finally agreed they would be allowed free passage providing they were not accompanied by any gentlemen.

Their attitude to dog breeding was one which, sadly, would not be accepted today. As long as it looked like a Deerhound and a good Deerhound at that, they were not too bothered if its ancestry was not known. In the 1920s they travelled around Ireland searching for stock and as a result of this some of their dogs were from unregistered stock. One has only to guess at what could well be behind many such dogs.

Ch. Tragic of Ross was in part the result of stock gathered from their searches and it is said that every kennel of his day owed something to him. He was the father of Aesthetic, so the grandfather of Prothetic. In an age when it was considered 'not the thing' to over-show Deerhounds, Prothetic won 11 CCs. Before the outbreak of war he headed a fine team of Deerhounds which the renowned American

sculptress, Anna Hyatt Huntingdon, took with her to the States.

Undoubtedly the best known piece in the Kennel Club's collection is the life-size bronze of the Foxhound *(Plate 58)*. This particular model was cast in 1925 and for many years stood over the porch of 84 Piccadilly and became a landmark in the West End of London. When the Club took over 1-4 Clarges Street in 1956 the hound moved to its new home in the entrance to the building.

Sculpted by Adrian Jones (1845-1938) it was modelled on Forager, a prize winning Foxhound of the Pytchley kennel. Forager belonged to Earl Spencer and was known as the classical type. He was modelled at Althorpe and Lord Annaly, who succeeded Lord Spencer as Master of the Pytchley, wrote to Jones on Christmas Day, 1893 'My Dear Jones, ... how delighted I am with the model you have made of Forager. It is really splendid and does you the greatest credit. You have the dog to the life and the work is beautifully artistic.....' There were castings of Forager in varying sizes and in silver as well as bronze.

Jones was an artist and sculptor who exhibited sculpture at the Royal Academy. He served as an Army Veterinary Captain and was a keen sportsman. Among his monumental sculptures is the large monument at the top of Constitution

Plate 60 Carved wooden model of Lady Dankwerts Whippet, Ch.Brekin Spode.
7" high. Spode was Best in Show at Leicester 1948.

Plate 61 Dr. Sidney Turner, Sculpt. The ideal Mastiff's head.

Hill at Hyde Park Corner called 'Peace in her Quadriga'.

A recent addition to the collection is a bronze of the Boxer, Ch.Wardrobes Miss Mink *(Plate 59)*. It was presented to the Kennel Club by Len Hammond on behalf of Mr. & Mrs.Wilson Wiley. Miss Mink was owned and bred by the Wileys, was the fourth Boxer to go Best in Show all breeds at a championship show and she was one of the most successful Boxers ever in all-breed competition. Sired by Ch.Winkinglight Justice out of Wardrobes Silver Spurs, she was only ever once beaten in her class and this was by her sister, Ch.Wardrobes Miss Sable. This was at Crufts in 1957 when she was tipped to win Best in Show. Many considered her the greatest Boxer ever and for many years she held the breed record with 27 CCs. She was the dam of three champions, including Ch.Wardrobes Wild Mink, sire of 11 champions.

The model of Miss Mink is by Doris Lindner (1896-1979) who had studied sculpture in London and Rome and was considered a great draughtswoman and worked always from life. She is known best for her work for Royal Worcester and modelled over 50 dogs for the company. She also had work cast in bronze by Heredities and accepted private commissions, of which Miss Mink is one. Miss Lindner used to travel to Wardrobes where Miss Mink was

brought in to the kitchen and stood on the kitchen table whilst the artist worked on her model.

As an art form, particularly in dog art, carved wooden figures are frequently not held in the esteem which some deserve. Our minds are clouded by mass produced St.Bernards with their barrels and Pekingese with their puppies. There are a few, the quality of which can rival other mediums and the Kennel Club have three such examples which represent three generations of Whippets owned by Lady Dankwerts. The unfortunate thing about carvings in wood is that, in the main, little is known about the carvers and such pieces are rarely fully signed, as is the case here, each just being signed 'DH'.

As Mrs.F.M.Dankwerts, she had been interested in a number of breeds pre-war and was perhaps best known in Dandie Dinmont Terrier circles. In 1944 she purchased from Mrs.Conway-Evans as a pet, Crusader of Conevan and subsequently 'borrowed' as a companion for Crusader, his white sister, White Statue of Conevan. White Statue became a champion and from her came in direct descent a line of outstanding bitches, including her daughter, Ch.Brekin Spode *(Plate 60)* and Spode's daughter, Ch.Brekin Ballet Shoes. It is these three, portrayed in painted wood, each 7" high, which are now in the Kennel Club collection. Spode did some spectacular winning, including Best in Show at Leicester in 1948 and the Hound Group at the Ladies Kennel Association show.

Lady Dankwerts was the daughter of the Rev.Dr.James Pride, rector of Bridlington, Yorkshire. Her husband, the Rt.Hon.Sir Harold Dankwerts, who was knighted in 1949, was at one time Lord Justice of Appeal. He too had an interest in dogs, being a member of the Kennel Club and president of the National Whippet Association.

A number of gifted artists have been members of the Kennel Club, none more prominent than Dr.Sidney Turner, one time chairman of the Committee of the Kennel Club. He was noted for his skill in modelling dogs' heads and these he had cast in bronze. One such example has recently been on loan to the Kennel Club from his granddaughter and is a fine example of a

Mastiff's head *(Plate 61)*. Turner was a prominent breeder of Mastiffs, among other breeds, was a founder member in 1883 of the Old English Mastiff Club and was one of those responsible for drawing up the standard description of the breed.

The drafting committee paid particular attention to defining the correct head of which the doctor's Ch.Orlando and Ch.Hotspur were considered outstanding in that respect. They failed in soundness, Orlando being described as "a cripple". Turner's bronze may well represent one of these two dogs but is most certainly an example of what he and fellow committee members, Rev.W.J.Mellor and Mr.W.K.Taunton, would have considered the ideal Mastiff head.

Nick Waters

Plate 62 The Board Room with its George III style furniture, where important decisions are made. On the side wall hang portraits of past chairmen and on the end wall hangs Terence Cuneo's portrait of Her Majesty The Queen, flanked by Maud Earl's study of the Rev. R. O'Callaghan's Irish Setters and Frank Paton's 'The Card Game'.

Plate 63 Gentlemen's Smoke Room. A George III mahogany sofa table, the crossbanded rounded rectangular top over a pair of frieze drawers upon solid trestle ends united by a ring turned tapered stretcher.

Plate 65 Board Room. An 18th century mahogany eight day longcase clock, the brass chapter ring with roman numerals. The clock's trunk is flanked by free-standing columns and ram's head masks and the pedestal base has carved feathers and claw feet. The longcase clock is one of the most valuable single pieces of furniture in the Kennel Club.

Plate 64 Lady Members Sitting Room. A 19th century French boulle and brass mounted bureau plat of rectangular serpentine shape with female figure mounts and claw sabots to the scrolled legs.

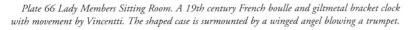

Plate 66 Lady Members Sitting Room. A 19th century French boulle and giltmetal bracket clock with movement by Vincentti. The shaped case is surmounted by a winged angel blowing a trumpet.

S. & J. Fuller (Publishers).
'Making a dash with a gay
Tilbury, your friend
recognises a Brother
Officer not famous for his
beauty, and with him a
very dashing lass; in the
endeavour to gain her
attention you DISCOVER
you have overlooked a
small Post on your whip
hand'.
Coloured aquatint,
7¹/₂" x 10¹/₂",
published Jan. 1st 1817 by
S. & J. Fuller ,
34 Rathbone Place.

Making a dash with a gay Tilbury, your friend recognizes a Brother Officer not famous for his beauty, and with him a very dashing Lass, in the endeavour to gain her attention you DISCOVER you have overlooked a small Post on your whip hand

London Pub. Jan.l 1817, by S. & J.Fuller, 34. Rathbone Place.

John James Chalon, RA
(after) (1778-1854).
'Les Tondeuses de Chiens'.
Chalon exhibited both
landscape and genre
subjects of great merit and
interest. They were
considered original both in
their conception and
treatment.
Hand coloured aquatint, 6
¹/₂" x 8¹/₂",
published May 1st 1820
by Rodwell and Martin,
New Bond St.

Designed & drawn on Stone by J.J.Chalon.

LES TONDEUSES DE CHIENS.

London Published by Rodwell & Martin, New Bond St. May 1. 1820.
C. Hullmandel's Lithography.

George Cruikshank (after) (1792-1878). 'Monstrosities 1821'. From illustrating children's books, Cruikshank turned his attention to satire and caricature, in particular ridiculing the follies of the fast young men of London. Hand coloured etching, 10" x 13½", published 1821 by G. Humphrey, 14 St. James's St.

Edward Irvine Halliday (b.1902). Evelyn, Lady Auckland of Cromlix. The prefix, Cromlix was famous for field trial gundogs both before and after the Second World War. Signed and dated 1934, oil on canvas, 25" x 30".

53

The General Committee of the Kennel Club which approved the idea of "Treasures of the Kennel Club"
Standing (L-R) Eric Smethurst, Keith Young, Valerie Foss, Esmèe Samuel, Ronnie Irving, Ann Bliss, Bill Hardaway,
John Banbury, Gillian Averis, John Clifford, Bernard Hall, Mason Minns, Ann Arch, Terry Thorn, Norman Ziman, Ruth Barbour,
Liz Cartledge, Irene Terry, Peter Meanwell.
Seated (L-R) Mike Stockman, Sybil Churchill, Peter Mann (vice-chairman), Peter James (chairman),
Roger French (chief executive and secretary), Jean Lanning and Ed Simpson.

(Two other members of the General Committee, Margaret Everton and Harry Hardwicke, were unable to be present on this occasion).

The men who have led from 1873 to 2000

Sewallis Evelyn Shirley

Chairman of the Kennel Club 1873-1899.
President of the Kennel Club 1899-1904.

Sewallis Evelyn Shirley who founded the Kennel Club in 1873 was a man of his time. In a competition to find who was the greatest of the Kennel Club's chairmen he would be a strong contender for first place. He was an aristocrat and extremely wealthy. In the book *The Great Landowners of Great Britain and Ireland,* S.E.S.' father is down as owning:-

26,386 acres in County Monaghan,

1,769 acres in Warwickshire,

605 acres in Worcestershire.

An annual ground valuation then of £23,744 translated into today's values will give an idea of their wealth.

The family was of Saxon descent. Sir Robert Shirley in 1677 succeeded to the Barony of Ferrers of Chartley and in 1711 was created Earl Ferrers and Viscount Tamworth. Earl Ferrers alienated the Ettington Estate from the elder line of the family, entailing it upon his eldest son of his second marriage, whose grandson, Evelyn John Shirley, was the father of S.E. Shirley.

S.E.S. was born in 1844, educated at Eton and Christ Church, Oxford. Interested in all country pursuits he had a pack of Beagles at Eton, rode to hounds, was an excellent shot, was interested in breeding dogs and worked his gun dogs .

In 1865 he exhibited his Fox Terriers at the Birmingham Dog Show Society Show. Dog shows preceded field trials by six years and the 14 years between the date of the first dog show and the foundation of the Kennel Club had seen many irregularities arise. If the sport was to continue with the right sort of people wishing to take part the need for legislation and guidance became a necessity. A body with power to enforce decisions for dogs needed to be brought into existence, just as the Jockey Club controlled equine affairs. The young S.E. was a man involved not only in all aspects of dogs but also government for he was an M.P. from 1868 to 1880, a Justice of the Peace and also High Sheriff and Deputy Lieutenant for County Monaghan. Obviously S.E. liked the idea of show competition with his dogs. On February 2, 1869, the National Dog Club was started, a society whose first and only show was held in June, 1869. Not a financial success, the club practically collapsed after the event and so it was not easy to get together another committee who would run a show in or near London. However, S.E. was determined and a show was arranged by S.E. and J.H. Murchison with an aristocratic and dog interested committee. It was held at the Crystal Palace in June, 1870. The show was a success in all respects but financially and the committee bore the monetary loss. Many of the committee declined to arrange a second show for the following year but S.E. carried on and the show was held, dog wise a success but again a financial disaster though less than the previous year.

It was inconvenient to have a meetings, different committee and officers each year for these early Crystal Palace shows. There was no permanent secretary, no funds, no regular office, no regular staff and S.E. realised if he and his friends were to carry on with this interesting hobby it had to be organised. S.E. was a member of the best clubs in London. What about an exclusive Kennel Club, to organise and run this new hobby?

Twelve other gentlemen met with him at 2 Albert Mansions, Victoria St, London on April 4, 1873, namely Mr F. Adock, Mr C.W. Hodge, Mr G. Brewis, Mr T.W. Hazelhurst, Col. Platt, Mr H.T. Mendal, Mr S. Lang, Mr Whitehouse, Mr Lort, Rev.J.C. Macdona, Viscount Hill and Mr J.H. Hawes. According to *The History Of*

The Birmingham Dog Show Society by Annette Oliver the majority of these were all associated at some time with the Birmingham Dog Show Society and so had the expertise required.

Picture from boardroom of the founder, first chairman and first president of the Kennel Club. The picture was subscribed for by Mr Shirley's many friends on his resignation of the chairmanship and was painted by Mr Stuart Wortley. Mr Shirley is in Kennel Club dress, seated in the dining room at Ettington with the fine oak panels and coats of arms of the family as a background. One of his famous Flatcoats is looking up at his master. English School, oil on canvas, 48¹/₂" x 36¹/₂"

The Kennel Club's first show took place at the Crystal Palace on June 17/18/19/20, 1873. There were 975 entries and the show was a success. From reading early minutes S.E. had some clever ideas which were soon put into practice. The Stud Book and Code of Rules for Shows and Trials gave who ever controlled them control of the emerging show and trial world. The first Kennel Club Stud Book covering shows and trials from 1859 to 1873 was distributed on the first day of the Birmingham Show, December 1, 1874. The Prince of Wales became the club's first patron and on his accession to the throne continued his patronage. The club's membership was limited to 100. For 26 years S.E. was chairman of the Kennel Club, and it was in 1884 that he married Miss Emily Macdonald, eldest daughter of Col. and the Honourable Mrs Macdonald of St Martins Abbey, Perthshire. The Kennel Club presented them with a silver gilt centre piece and a loving cup of 18th century plate. Two years earlier his father had died and S.E. had inherited Ettington Park, near Stratford-on-Avon and Lough Fea, Co Monaghan.

In 1880 S.E. had founded the *Kennel Gazette* which was originally his private property. It was a great success and in 1881 S.E. handed it over to the Kennel Club. In 1899 on resigning as chairman. S.E. was elected first president of the Kennel Club, the position he held until his death in 1904.

S.E. was the complete dog man. One of the most famous judges of his day, he first judged in 1873. Not only did he judge at all shows in the United Kingdom but also in Russia, France and Belgium. He was a well known field trial judge of Setters and Pointers and an excellent shot, who enjoyed working his own dogs. Being both breeder and exhibitor he kept a large kennels at Ettington.

His Flatcoated Retriever kennel was dominant in the 1880s and it was quite usual to hear a Wavy Coated Retriever (later called Flat-coated) referred to as a 'Shirley Retriever'. He loved his Flatcoats and sought to improve the breed regardless of time or expense. He wanted to maintain and improve its capacity in the field as well as to fix a type which would satisfy his ideals.

His famous dogs were Paris, Ch Zelstone, a famous sire whom he bought from Mr Farquharson, Ch Moonstone, Ch Hopeful, Ch Wiseacre, Ch Sloe, Ch Zee, and Ch Tacit and from his great dogs are descended the dogs of Harding Cox, Allan Shuter, Col Cornwall Legh, Lord Redesdale, H Reginald Cooke and directly on to the great Flatcoats of the last 20 years. He had champion English Setters and Pointers, Bulldogs, Bull Terriers, Fox Terriers and Collies. One has to say that S.E. Shirley was a man of his time and a sentence from his obituary is his best description. *"A truer sportsman, a keener judge, and a better example of what an English country gentleman should be could not be found."* S.E. Shirley and the early history of the Kennel Club are the same thing. From when he first conceived the idea of evolving law and order out of the chaos which then surrounded the exhibition of dogs, his personal influence enabled him to form the first committee of the Kennel Club. The success of the undertaking was largely due to his tact, discretion and judgement. Very much a leader of men he gave his careful consideration to all club affairs. His great experience, wisdom and foresight was brought into play when difficult and delicate questions had to be decided. In early March, 1904, S.E. Shirley left the Kennel Club to go to look at a black Pomeranian he was anxious to buy for his wife. On the way he had a seizure and died. The news of his death was brought to the Kennel Club soon after.

The magnificent Ettington Park where he lived is now a luxurious country house hotel. In the park stands the old church for the village but the only parts remaining are the tower and south transept which became the chapel of Ettington Park and, since 1825, the burying place of the family. Here Sewallis Evelyn Shirley was buried.

J. Sidney Turner, Chairman of the Kennel Club 1899-1920
English School, oil on canvas, 34³/₄" x 36"

Dr John Sydney Turner

Chairman of the Kennel Club 1899-1920

Dr J Sydney Turner was the ideal man to follow S.E. Shirley as chairman. He had a high profile in dogs at the time. Born in 1843 he was educated at Merchant Taylor's School and at Guy's Hospital where he went on to become house surgeon. He was a magistrate and held many public offices. He first exhibited dogs in 1862, originally Bull Terriers and Black and Tan Terriers and then many breeds. But by the late 1800s he concentrated on Mastiffs and Bloodhounds in which breeds he had great success and was an acknowledged authority. He was a founder member of the Old English Mastiff Club and helped to produce the first breed standard.

At this time the Mastiff was a popular show dog. Sydney Turner's were some of the greatest, including the outstanding Ch Beaufort and among many other champions the lovely Ch Orlando. His Bloodhounds produced Ch Triumph, Ch Lord Raglan, Ch Trinket and Ch Wardle Welcome among others. As a judge he was one of the greatest of his day. He was author of many medical tracts and dogwise he edited the authoritative *Kennel Encyclopaedia*. Should you possess a perfect set in parts or correctly bound into four volumes of the *Kennel Encyclopaedia* you have a valuable part of

cynological literature. Turner was first elected a member of the Kennel Club Committee in 1886. Probably the most artistic of the KC chairmen, he modelled dogs in wax which were then cast in bronze. He modelled a superb Mastiff head *(Plate 61)*, now in the possession of his grand-daughter who lent the Kennel Club the most interesting memorial scrapbook. Sydney Turner's wife was a member of the Ladies' Branch of the Kennel Club.

Some things that were attended to during his years of office as chairman were: banning cropped dogs from being shown; fixing the standard type for breeds, and in words stating the points of their particular breeds in a concise form and printed for the guidance of judges, exhibitors and the general public; saw the codification of the Kennel Club rules; covered the question of the infected dogs being shown; saw that entries closed at a fixed date. During his term of office many other important rules went through. Sydney Turner died when he was 76 years old and had been chairman of the Kennel Club for 21 years.

Mark Hanbury Beaufoy

Chairman of the Kennel Club 1920-1922

Mr Beaufoy was born in 1854 and educated at Eton and Cambridge and while an undergraduate first became interested in dogs. His two breeds were Bloodhounds and Mastiffs. In Bloodhounds he had Ch Nestor (black and tan, the Stud Book says, specifically no white) The Mastiff had its peak of popularity during the period 1870-1883 when Mr Beaufoy was an active breeder and exhibitor.

Mark Beaufoy, Chairman of the Kennel Club 1920-1922

He owned Ch Nero later in his career and bred and owned Ch Beau a fawn dog who was an influential stud. Mark Beaufoy became a member of the Kennel Club in 1878, joining the committee a year later but then that same year resigned from the commitee and also his membership. In 1886 he contested the

Kennington Division of Lambeth as a Liberal and although unsuccessful was elected at the by-election of 1889, retaining the seat until 1895 when he was defeated owing to a difference with the Temperance Party. In 1888 he removed his kennels to his country seat Coombe, near Shaftesbury, but finding not enough time to attend them properly his dogs were sold off at the Kennel Club show of 1891.

In 1904 he once again became a member of the Kennel Club and in 1905 was re-elected to the committee. In 1910 he was elected vice-chairman. At the meeting of the General Committee, March, 1920, Mr Beaufoy was unanimously elected chairman to fill the vacancy caused by J. Sydney Turner's death. He was valued for his performance of the duties of his office and his commanding knowledge of business. On November 10, 1922, he died at the age of 68. Mark Beaufoy was the antithesis to the first and second chairmen of the Kennel Club, such large figures in all aspects of the dog world. He was involved in the complete re-drafting of the Kennel Club rules but his period in office was too short for him to really make a mark. He died whilst in office.

Francis Redmond

Chairman of the Kennel Club 1922-1925

Francis Redmond was one of the most popular dog men of his day. His education and upbringing were different from that of the previous three chairmen, but he was definitely one of nature's gentlemen. He became a member of the Kennel Club in 1882 and in 1893 was elected on to the committee. In 1904 he was given the great honour of being made one of the three trustees of the club. He was vice chairman before becoming chairman.

Francis Redmond was born in 1843, the son of a publican father. He grew up a true sportsman, fond of hunting and shooting and for many years a regular follower of the Old Berkeley Foxhounds and the Berkhampstead Staghounds. He also had a famous loft of homing pigeons. It gives an idea how influential Francis Redmond was in the breeding of Smooth Fox Terriers that between 1891 and 1921 he won the Fox Terrier Club Challenge Trophy 24 times.

Francis Redmond did not have an affix but his dogs all had names beginning with the letter

'D'. He started in pedigree dogs in 1869 and was one of the original committee of the Fox Terrier Club formed in 1876. He helped to draw up the standard and type to which to breed and it was so well worded by the committee, with their qualifications in hunting and with horse backgrounds (one of the committee, John A. Doyle M.H., bred Rosedrop, winner of the Oaks and dam of Gainsborough who won the 1918 Derby) that it is almost unaltered today. He was also president of the Fox Terrier Club, at a time when the Fox Terrier was at the top of its popularity as a show dog. Mr Redmond bred 14 Smooth F.T. Champions and owned another nine. He bred five Wire F.T. champions and owned one Wire champion. His influence in Smooths was far greater than just the number of champions he bred or owned for his champions were considered to be among the best. He became a judge of great repute and was honoured by the American Fox Terrier Club when he visited America to judge its first specialty show at Newport, Rhode Island, in 1885. He had an entry of 75 Smooths and four Wires, his decisions and opinions carried an authority never attained before or since and it was said that "If Redmond put a dog up, then his value increased immediately by £50." He was a most outspoken man who called a spade a spade. During the 1923 dinner of the Fox Terrier Club he spoke out about breeding systems and favoured 'like begets like' and maintained that a knowledge of the faults and virtues of their ancestors was necessary. It was the last speech he made for he was taken ill several days after the meeting and never fully recovered.

"The 'golden decade' for the kennel was in the 1890s. Mr Redmond commissioned several paintings by Arthur Wardle of the terriers he had during that time, the most famous being the Totteridge Eleven, and there were portraits of Ch. Donna Fortuna, Ch Dame Fortune and Ch Duchess of Durham as well. However, if we look at actual photographs of his dogs we can see how his stud dogs were important in the evolution of the long elegant Fox Terrier head from the deeper stopped head that is still carried today by the Parson Russell Terrier.

Ch Dominie, born in 1887, had a head of the really old fashioned type (though it was substantially upgraded in the portrait) but Mr Redmond's Terriers soon had the longer leaner heads, and by 1912 Ch D'Orsay's model had an almost modern shape.

Ch Dominie's claim to fame is as the sire of the phenomenal bitch Ch Donna Fortuna. Before she was 7 months old she had won the CC at Crufts (in 1898). Shown consistently for five years she was never beaten, having won the bitch CC from the veteran class at the Fox Terrier Club's show.

Mr J.H. Pardoe knew Mr Redmond's kennels and wrote, "Perhaps it is because in my youth I hunted with the same hounds in Hertfordshire as Francis Redmond, a special glamour is attached in my mind to his Totteridge kennels. But the fact remains that to me there has never been a terrier of such superlative merit as his Donna Fortuna, and whenever I want to refresh my mind as to what a Fox Terrier should really be, I turn to the incomparable picture of that great bitch, born 53 years ago in July 1896."

Once her show career was finished she was put in the care of a game keeper, who in two months had her broken and working with ferrets. Mr J.C. Tinne, another founder of the club, wrote in 1903 "She goes down in posterity as absolutely the best Fox Terrier of all time."

It is still possible to see her today in the Natural History Museum collection at Tring, Hertfordshire.

The Kennel Gazette started in 1881, had an opening article on "fashionable kennels", those of Mr Redmond. This commented that "there is nothing more difficult to breed than a first class Fox Terrier, and competition is rendered more keen from the fact that the breed is now excessively well understood, and the critics include some excellent judges of animal formation generally, and are almost super-critical over the points and perfections of a Fox Terrier. Among those who have been fairly successful may be ranked Mr F. Redmond, who commenced the formation of his kennel 12 years ago, but it was some little time before he could get into the winning strain, as at first he bought his experience in the same way others have done, by accepting too much what is seen at shows, without using judgement to discern the pure from the spurious. A total change was necessary, and a few judicious purchases furnished the material to ensure the probability of success. Legs and feet, just like Foxhounds, should be pattern to follow, and on this point Mr Redmond is crotchety".

It was universally agreed that Mr Redmond was responsible for the good feet and legs found in the breed. He was a very popular chairman of the Kennel Club, though towards the end his health made attendance difficult. At a meeting on February 3, 1925, the committee accepted with very deep regret the resignation of Francis Redmond as chairman. In a letter he expressed his great regret at resigning, but explained that he felt now that the club's affairs were again in a thoroughly satisfactory condition it was a favourable opportunity for him to make way for younger blood to help carry on what the club had done and was doing to uphold the character and the dignity of the canine world.

Francis Redmond, Chairman of the Kennel Club 1922-1925 Mouat Loudan, signed and dated 1925, oil on cnavas, 40' x 30'

He expressed his indebtedness to the committee and to Mr Boswell, the secretary, for their able and loyal support which had lightened his responsibilities and had made his position a pleasure. He hoped, when his health permitted, to resume his attendance at the meetings. Francis Redmond was made a Vice – President of the club.

He appeared outwardly stern but had a good sense of humour. When he became interested in Wire Fox Terriers he bought a dog named Daytime and renamed him (it could be done in those days) "The Untrimmed", which reflected the Kennel Club's rule forbidding any trimming of the coat. Shortly afterwards the rule was modified to permit a little tidying and Redmond changed the dog's name to "The Reclaimed". Redmond always contended that trimming had a strong influence on judges.

The last Redmond champion was the homebred Ch Dusky Doris, born in 1921 and made up in 1922. When Mr Redmond died a dispersal sale was held on April 7, 1927, at the Crystal Palace, with the proceeds going to the Fox Terrier Club. The Rev Rosslyn Bruce reported that "Nearly all the committee and most of the members of the club were present, in recognition both of their respect for the late president and of his generosity in bequeathing his kennel to the club. Besides them, many of Redmond's personal friends came, as did also a large number of others interested in so unusual a gathering.

At the beginning of the sale a few onlookers, ignorant of the depth of sentiment that attached to the occasion, expressed surprise at the prices paid, but they soon realised this sale was an expression of practical devotion to an old friend and his favourites. A true gentleman sportsman Redmond handled his own dogs in the ring, until ill health caused him to use other handlers. A great sporting amateur, he also had a keen sense of business. He sold dogs for what in those days were huge sums of money, Ch. Dame Fortune was sold for £300 and he was supposed to have sold a champion Smooth to India for a reputed £1000. He twice refused £500 for Ch Donna Fortuna. His dogs also reaped huge amounts of prize money. There is still a very personal link left with Francis Redmond, for Peter and Francis Winfield of the famous Riber Smooth Fox Terriers have the light chain lead owned and used by Francis Redmond on his famous dogs.

How did the Winfields get the chain? On Redmond's death it went to Captain Tudor Crosthwaite, who left the famous Redmond painting "The Totteridge Eleven" to the Kennel Club. From Crosthwaite's kennelman it went to Capt. John Glover, involved in Smooth Fox Terriers for over 60 years and he judged the Fox Terrier Club's centenary show. It was given to the Winfields who used it on the last dog they showed, Riber Redmond (pet name John, not Francis!).

Francis Redmond died in early 1927 aged 84 years. At the Kennel Club annual meeting on March 4 reference was made to his death. and a resolution of condolence was passed to his sister, Mrs Talbot with the members of the committee present upstanding.

William Lesley McCandlish

Chairman of the Kennel Club 1925-1935

In the spirit of the first, second and fourth chairmen. William Lesley McCandlish was known throughout the dog world as breeder, exhibitor, judge, author and administrator. The son of a prominent Scottish advocate, he was educated in Edinburgh and went into business

W. L. McCandlish, Chairman of the Kennel Club 1925-1935
Alfred Egerton Cooper, signed, oil on canvas, 40" x 30"

with the Scottish Widows insurance company in 1892. He then moved to Bristol and married, in 1899, Millicent Fry, a member of the famous chocolate manufacturing family. Although he had started to show Scottish Terriers in 1892 many moves had made it impossible to start breeding but now, settled near Bristol with his wife, he started what was to become the legendary Ems strain. He had known the Scottish Terrier in its earliest days before recognition by the Kennel Club and could tell much about its origin. In 1903 he became secretary of the Scottish Terrier Club (England) and held that post until 1914 and was later its president.

Few people have ever devoted so much time, care and thought over a long period to the welfare of a breed as did McCandlish for the Scottish Terrier. He wrote with authority and charm, and his monograph on the breed, together with innumerable articles published, did much to foster its interests and increase its popularity. He founded his kennel on three good bitches, all of which became champions.

He bought Seafield Beauty from her breeder, Mr Andrew Kinnear, after she had started her show career, and she became a champion in 1903. Next foundation was Ch Ems Enya, bred by Mr R. Puller and who gained her title in 1904. Last of the trio was Ch Ems Music, bred by Mr Robert Chapman senior, founder of the

Heather Kennel which reached great heights in the inter-war period when run by his two sons.

The first homebred champion was Ch Ems Cosmetic, title 1905, who was painted by Arthur Wardle. In all Mr McCandlish bred 11 champions, and there was also the bought-in Ch Ems Chevalier. The last Ems champion was Ch Ems Quisby, made up in 1913, as the First World War brought the breeding programme to an end. The great rival of the Heather kennel in the 1930's was that of Mr Cowley's Albournes, indeed these two kennels could be considered the foundation of the modern show breed world-wide, and the Albournes were based on Ems bloodlines.

Though Ch Ems Morning Nip is recorded in the Stud Book as grey brindle it was noted elsewhere that he was the first wheaten champion, "his harsh dense jacket was the colour of ripe corn, tipped with black. He scored in clean skull, eye placement, ears and expression with big bones."

When he and his wife moved to Worcestershire W.L. McCandlish became a director of the Bromsgrove Guild of Fine Arts, the firm which did a lot of the ornamental metal work of the railings of Buckingham Palace and for the London Passenger Transport Board on some of the Underground stations. The 1914 – 1918 war halted breeding operations and by the end he had no bitches left of his famous Ems line. McCandlish was in great demand as a judge and he judged at most championship shows in the British Isles. He also judged in America. He hated exaggerations in all forms and although he withheld CCs on five occasions he was held in high esteem by the dog world and judged the Scottish Terrier Club (England) first championship show in 1918.

He was the author of the first book on the Scottish Terrier breed, the standard work for many years. His other book, *Popular Dog Show Maxims – Judges, Judged and Judging*, published in 1926, still has many bearings on today's dog world. One paragraph from it reads:

"For his own mental clarity, as well as for the benefit of the onlookers, the system by which a judge gradually discards is one of the best. Without explaining his reasons he should steadily unfold to the spectator the product of his brain. This not only makes judging interesting to the experienced, but materially helps the education of the novice, or dog breeding would soon develop into the industry of taking in each other's washing. Although the experienced judge varies his procedure according to the numbers and quality of the dogs before him, the less experienced should stick to the method he has decided to adopt before hand, and the opening move is of importance. The nervousness of starting is recovered from if a sound and simple opening formula is adopted".

Excellent in the managerial department of shows, he started as secretary in Bristol and became chairman of Bristol Kennel Club until 1906. In 1920 he was on the committee of management of the Birmingham Dog Show Society. He had been elected a member of the Kennel Club in 1902 and in 1905 was elected to the General Committee. In 1922 he became vice-chairman of the committee and in the last year of Francis Redmond's chairmanship he chaired many of the meetings. On the resignation of Francis Redmond, the general committee unanimously elected McCandlish as chairman. He was an excellent administrator and his years in office saw much sensible and easily worked canine legislation go through.

In March 1935 George Howlett became chairman of the Kennel Club and a vote of thanks was passed on to W.L. McCandlish for the services he had rendered the club. He was a trustee of the Kennel Club and became a vice-president, an office he kept to his death. He was exceedingly interested in gundog work and was a good shot. He officiated as a judge at trials and of the many committees he sat on one was the K.C. Field Trial and Management Committee. He died on June 29, 1947. when aged 79.

G. D. Howlett, 1927 Chairman of the Kennel Club 1935-1937

Mr George D. Howlett.

Chairman of the Kennel Club 1935 - 1937

George Howlett was born in 1874 and enjoyed the later part of his education at the Lycee de Caen in Normandy. He served abroad in the South African war and joined the Kennel Club in 1912, being elected a member of the General Committee in 1919. In 1922 he was appointed one of the trustees and in 1928 was elected unanimously as vice-chairman. On March 19, 1935 he was elected chairman with the well known breeder, judge and author, Arthur Croxton-Smith, as his vice-chairman.

It was during George Howlett's chairmanship that the allocation of challenge certificates to each breed and based upon the number of registrations in each breed during a specified 12 months was agreed.

George Howlett presided at the annual general meeting in March, 1937, but by the Bi-Annual General Meeting in October that year A. Croxton-Smith had been elected chairman of the committee. Thanks were expressed by the committee to Howlett who continued to be a trustee and serve on the executive and shows committees, though later in the year he expressed his desire to relinquish membership of the show committee owing to increasing pressure of business. A resolution expressing the committee's gratitude for, and appreciation of, his invaluable services on the show committee, of which he had been a member since 1920 and of which he had been chairman for 17 years, was carried with acclamation. George Howlett died in 1942.

He was a Wire Fox Terrier breeder and exhibitor, breeding three champions and owning another four during the late 1920's and the 1930s, a time when the Wire had taken over from the Smooth as the most popular and competitive breed. As Tom Horner wrote "this was the golden age of the Wire. The breed topped the registrations and the competition was of the highest. Professional handlers abounded and it was almost unheard of for an owner to handle his own dog to win a challenge certificate let alone make it a champion".

Mr Howlett's terriers came from the most popular bloodlines, based firmly on the Duchess of Newcastle's line and using the cream of the available stud dogs. His most successful champion was Ch Kemphurst Superb, the winner of 11 CCs and best in show at the Kennel Club's own show in 1927. She was bred by Mr Bob Barlow, probably the greatest Terrier man ever, at his Crackley Kennels. Another champion brought in was Ch Kemphurst Creole who was by Ch Talavera Simon the most influential Wire sire then and, possibly, of all time. The homebred Ch Kemphurst Carnation was a daughter of Ch Beau Brummell of

Wildoaks as was Ch Kemphurst Culliud Gal. Ch Kemphurst Confectionery was a daughter of Ch Crackley Startler, a son of Beau Brummell.

George Howlett was a popular terrier judge and considered to have outstanding ability. He had judging assignments all over Europe and America and was president of the Wire Fox Terrier Association in 1922.

A. Croxton-Smith OBE, *Chairman of the Kennel Club 1937-1948*
T. Dugdale, signed, oil on canvas, 36" x 31¼"

Arthur Croxton Smith OBE

Chairman of the Kennel Club 1937-1948

Arthur Croxton Smith, always known as 'A Croxton Smith', came from Huntingdonshire and a family which had been involved with land for generations and so, it was written in 1935, "he took naturally to dog breeding." Croxton Smith, born in 1865, was educated privately and when old enough was articled to the *Northampton Mercury and Daily Record*. He moved to London as a young man and was appointed assistant editor of *The Gentlewoman*, but left in 1909 to take up article writing. Having a large exhibition kennel of dogs he soon specialised in this subject.

As a young man he had played football for Northampton, had been an athlete, had rowed, boxed, played lacrosse and lawn tennis, a game which he continued through most of his life.

His first dogs were Basset Hounds. Then Bloodhounds were added and Mr Croxton Smith was soon to become one of the founders of the Association of Bloodhound breeders.

He was elected chairman of the General Committee 36 years after his initial appointment to that committee in 1901 and some 40 years after becoming a Kennel Club member. At the time of his election to the chair it was recorded in the *Kennel Gazette,* "There are but few today who have greater experience both as a legislator and also as a canine expert ... Before the war his literary abilities were of the greatest service to the canine community and it is due to him that the important daily papers introduced dogs as a feature of news to their readers."

One of the papers for which he wrote was *The Daily Telegraph* and it is interesting to note that his career with the General Committee was not, in fact, continuous. He became a member of the Kennel Club in 1899, was elected to the General Committee in 1901, but retired in 1908. He was re-elected in 1920 and from then his service was continuous, being elected vice-chairman for the years 1935 and 1936 before taking over in the chair in 1937.

He was made a trustee of the Kennel Club in 1938 and remained so until 1952 when he resigned "to make way for a younger man." He had been made a vice-president of the club in 1948, the year he left the chair.

In the *Kennel Gazette* of January, 1949, Croxton Smith wrote, "John Bright described England as the mother of Parliaments, so may we claim that the Kennel Club is the mother of kennel clubs whose progeny, sometimes under other names, are to be found in many countries."

Croxton Smith was an erudite and distinguished writer who wrote in excess of 20 books on dogs and dog-related subjects and many articles for the canine press and magazines.

During the First World War he was Director of Publicity to the Ministry of Food and served on committees set up by the Cabinet in the post-war years to deal with the railway and coal strikes and the general strike of 1926.

He was chairman of the General Committee throughout the 1939-45 war and later wrote of that period, "In 1942 when I was chairman of the committee I had an additional duty to try to act as a very inadequate substitute for Buckley (E Holland Buckley, the secretary) who had joined the Forces."

The *Dog World Annual* of 1945 contains an article by Thomas Corbett, in which he wrote of the period under Croxton Smith's chairmanship and secretaryship, saying that the Kennel Club, though bombed and depleted of staff still ruled, however, with wise and far-seeing outlook. Shows were reduced to a minimum, consistent with a war-organised nation but the dog had established itself in the hearts of the people with many new adherents to the dog fancy crowding in.

Perhaps the *Kennel Gazette* best summed up Arthur Croxton Smith's service to the Kennel Club when it referred to it as "many years of valuable work and other interests which included posts as diverse as secretary of the Milk Publicity Council and chairman of Guide Dogs for the Blind." He died in August, 1952.

Air Commodore John Allan Cecil-Wright AFC, T.D., A.E.

Chairman of the Kennel Club 1948-1973

President of the Kennel Club 1976-1982

This was a man with a strong personality, with energy and enthusiasm, with positive ideas and a will and determination to see them carried through. He was also a man gifted with much foresight. In his Air Force days he had hanging in the mess, a newspaper headline which read "Sleep is just a waste of time".

At the Kennel Club he was always in command and with Ted Holland Buckley as secretary to Cecil-Wright's chairman, they made one of the finest combinations. As chairman he steered the club through many fundamental post-war changes, like the setting up of a Kennel Club inquiry office at general championship shows; like an attempt at better liaison with the press; at encouraging individual members to study fully the workings of the club, so that they could help with better public relations at shows and other canine occasions; like meeting with members of government, in order to be aware of any "doggy" legislation which may go through Parliament.

John Allan Cecil Wright was born August 28, 1886, (he changed his name by deed poll in 1957, to become Cecil-Wright). His father had a successful engineering business which became Warne, Wright and Rowland. Allan Cecil-Wright joined the company and was active until

63

retiring when well into his eighties. He served as chairman from 1920-1963.

He also had a distinguished career with the forces and, following the Armistice in 1918, together with Lord Brabazon of Tara, Col. Baldwin and F.N. Pickett, he was responsible for the German Shepherd Dog (or Alsatian as it was called for so many years) being introduced and established in this country. With his second wife, Lillian, he became deeply involved with what was always for him the Alsatian, she on the breeding and exhibiting and he on the administrative side. Their prefix was Louvencourt and in the early 20s they imported from Germany Kuno Von Brunnenhof, a

Air/Com J. A. Cecil-Wright AFC, TD, DL Chairman of the Kennel Club 1948-1973 William Dring, signed and dated 1956, oil on canvas, 36" x 31¼"

significant force in the breed in this country. He won five challenge certificates and sired Ch. Cuno of Louvencourt. Other successful dogs were Rudolf of Louvencourt, Phantom Wolf of Makinak, Coon of Louvencourt and UT21 of Oxenford. Cecil-Wright became interested in the working side of the breed and with Bordie of Cheyney he won at the association of Sheep, Police and Army Dog Society Working Trials in 1932. One of the 20 original members of The Alsatian League and Club of Great Britain, founded in 1924, he eventually became president. Cecil-Wright was also deeply interested in politics. In 1936 he became an M.P. but was defeated at the 1945 election. In 1946 he married Ethne Falconer who was very supportive in all his further dog activities. He had become a member of the Kennel Club in 1924 and was elected to the General Committee in 1935. He was the representative on the General Committee for Birmingham Dog Show Society for nearly 40 years and was on the Show Regulations and Working Trials Committees.

In 1948, on the retirement of A. Croxton Smith, he was elected chairman of the committee and in 1950 both the chairman and vice-chairman became ex-officio members of all the committees. He was elected a vice-president of the Club in 1973 and president (one of the few non-royals) in 1976. Other offices which he

held in the dog world included being a member of the executive committee of the Animal Health Trust, president of both Crufts and the Welsh Kennel Club and vice-president of both the Scottish Kennel Club and the National Canine Defence League. His allegiance and love of the Midlands extended to everything with which he became involved. He was president of Birmingham Dog Show Society and, with his wife, founding members of the Midland Counties Canine Society, later becoming president.

Cecil-Wright's interest in dogs extended to judging, the highlight was judging best in show at Crufts 1971 when 84 years old. His winner was Prince Ahmed Hussain's German Shepherd Ch. Ramacon Swashbuckler. Although very ill during the winter of 1981 he attended Crufts as president on the second day but this was his last public appearance at any Kennel Club function. He died a month short of his 96th birthday.

SIR RICHARD GLYN

Chairman of the Kennel Club 1973- 1976

Col Sir Richard Glyn had a short, three-year term of office which ended abruptly when he resigned and walked from a General Committee meeting in December, 1976. A statement issued at the time said he had resigned "on a point of principle" which, it was widely believed, was because the committee were at loggerheads over his wishes for a more democratic approach at the Kennel Club.

All this was at a time before women were admitted as full members of the Kennel Club and Sir Richard had supported the idea of a committee of inquiry to look into the issue. But then there was a sharp exchange of ideas concerning another matter within the committee and Sir Richard resigned and left.

Sir Richard's painting hangs in the Board Room at Clarges Street and is one of two by Terence Cuneo and, as is customary with Cuneo pictures, the "Cuneo mouse" (his trademark) can be found in the painting. It is above Sir Richard's left shoulder. The second Cuneo is of the Queen and her dogs and the mouse is to be found between the front legs of the black Labrador lying in front of her.

Sir Richard Glyn was born in 1907 of an old Dorset family. He joined the Kennel Club in 1934, being appointed to the General

Col. Sir Richard Glyn BT, OBE, TD, DL
Chairman of the Kennel Club 1973-1976.
Terence Cuneo (1907-1996) signed oil on canvas, 40" x 30"

Committee four years later. In 1958 he became its vice chairman and 15 years later, in 1973, was elected to the chair.

He had been appointed a trustee in 1963 and two years after his resignation he was made a vice-president.

He died in 1980 but during his life enjoyed a variety of careers. He practised as a barrister and had advised the General Committee on legal matters as well as writing articles in the *Kennel Gazette* on topics such as "The law as to dogs, their owners and keepers." He also farmed, was Member of Parliament for North Dorset for 13 years from 1957 and served on the Speaker's Conference on Electoral Law.

He additionally was active in the Territorial Army from 1927 and attained the rank of full colonel. For four years from 1958 to 1962 he was ADC to the Queen.

His canine interest was Bull Terriers and he founded a well-known kennel of coloured Bull Terriers. He used three affixes: Wuggins for the coloureds; Whitehot for the white Bull Terriers and Welterweight for his Miniature Bull Terriers.

He wrote a standard reference book on the breed and was editor and contributor with others of the book *Champion Dogs of the World.*

Among other dog-related interests he served on the Canine Consultative Council from its foundation in 1973, retiring as its chairman in 1979 on grounds of ill health. He resigned as a trustee of the Kennel Club in October 1980, shortly before his death.

LEONARD PAGLIERO

Chairman of the Kennel Club 1976-1981

"The chairmanship of the General Committee (of the Kennel Club) is a demanding, time-consuming job, more arduous than most people realise," said Leonard Pagliero, who for five years reigned as chairman. This statement is not untypical of many made by him, for he was described in one newspaper article as "a man of firm opinions."

In 1980 he took issue with the BBC over a programme on pedigree dogs, saying "This particular programme was a complete travesty, thoroughly prejudiced in its content and presentation and making no attempt to produce a balanced argument."

It was his determined stand over many issues which attracted criticism in certain sections of the dog press but which also achieved many things for the Kennel Club, not least of which was the creation of a series of world-wide conferences of kennel clubs from many countries. The first was hosted by the Kennel Club in London in 1978, two years after Leonard Pagliero came to office. He had joined the Kennel Club in 1957 and continued to become one of its longest serving members and holding the office of vice president along with a small number of other persons, some titled, all highly respected.

He was co-opted to a seat on the General Committee at a meeting on February 17, 1959 and was elected that committee's chairman 17 years later in December 1976, after the sudden resignation of Sir Richard Glyn 13 days earlier. Mr Pagliero was re-elected at each of the four succeeding annual elections but then came a decision not to offer himself for a further year when the committee met on July 7, 1981.

Much had been accomplished in the five years of his tenure of office and he publicly acknowledged "this had been made possible by the generous co-operation of his colleagues and loyal staff."

Mr John Taylor was quoted at the time as saying of Mr Pagliero "He has done a magnificent job in a period of change and expansion."

There were tributes to his hard work and leadership and criticism of those who had attacked Mr Pagliero and "not made his task easier." Mr Pagliero always maintained the Kennel Club had changed in his time from a social club first and an administration second to "business first and a social club second."

*Leonard Pagliero OBE, FCIS
Chairman of the
Kennel Club 1976-1981
Edward L. Halliday,
signed and dated 1980,
oil on canvas, 40" 30½"*

In a statement after his resignation he said, "I have been criticised. I am well aware I have not pleased everyone but I have done my best."

One who left the General Committee suddenly during Mr Pagliero's chairmanship was the late Group Captain A G (Beefy) Sutton. His surprise resignation from the General Committee in July, 1980, was explained by the group captain with the words, "For some time now I have been unable to go along with the methods of the chairman of the General Committee in a number of matters".

Leonard Pagliero was chairman of the General Committee when women were admitted to full membership of the Kennel Club (in 1979).

But their inclusion as full members was not straightforward. The Kennel Club had been taken to a tribunal by the late Mrs Florence Nagle in a fight not dissimilar to the way she had taken on the Jockey Club to obtain the right for women to become racehorse trainers.

Mrs Nagle lost the battle at the tribunal, but in its findings the tribunal indicated it had not been satisfied with the Kennel Club's attitude. Shortly afterwards the General Committee announced they were reconsidering the position and within weeks declared it would be in the best interests of the dog world at large if women became members of the club.

While the Kennel Club went through some turbulent years during the 1970s and 1980s there were advances which take a place in Kennel Club history. It was during Mr Pagliero's tenure of office that a computer satellite centre was opened at Maidenhead. While this was eventually closed and all records were brought back to Clarges Street, moves of this nature paved the way for other changes which were to be brought in during later years.

The series of world conferences of kennel clubs may not have achieved all that was hoped, perhaps because too many kennel clubs were intent on pursuing their own ideals, but at least there was discussion on a wide-ranging variety of dog-related topics and it was decided under Mr Pagliero's leadership of the KC that, as a guiding principle, breed standards should follow that of the country of origin of any breed of dog. This principle still applies.

His first love in dogs was German Shepherds, or Alsatians as he prefers to know them. But he is also known for his love of Beagles and in recent years has been assiduous in his support of the Hound Association, whose annual championship show at Stafford county showground regularly presents packs of working and former working hounds. Changes in social ideas have resulted in animals such as Otterhounds being removed from the working scene, but they can still be seen parading at HoundShow under the watchful eye of Leonard Pagliero.

JOHN ARNOTT MacDOUGALL
Chairman of the Kennel Club 1981-1996

In his 15 years as chairman John MacDougall instituted many changes at the Kennel Club, not least among them turning round a difficult financial situation and reducing criticism of its service to pedigree dogs.

Though, with his wife, Daphne, his main interest in dogs was the Miniature Poodles they bred under the Jolda affix, he held a number of offices in dog societies before being elected "the top man" in Britain. He had become a member of the Kennel Club in 1970 but it was another seven years before he first was to serve on the Administrative Committee and, finally, the

John MacDougall M CHIR FRCS
Chairman of the Kennel Club 1981-1996
John Edwards, signed, oil on canvas, 40" x 30"

General Committee in 1980. Twelve months later he was its chairman and one could say he was a "one-off" chairman.

The Field, in its August issue of 1981 headlined MacDougall's appointment as chairman, "The New Face Of The Kennel Club", subtitling its article, "John MacDougall and his role as guardian and guide."

Its opening paragraph succinctly sums up his appointment ... "Whatever undercurrents prompted the General Committee of the Kennel Club to go virtually outside their own ranks in electing John MacDougall their chairman, the effects potentially concern everybody who owns a pedigree dog.

Wilson Stephens, himself a member of the General Committee for ten years until 1977, the author of *The Field* article, wrote, "He attended his first General Committee meeting only last year. Now he has been made its chairman, elevated over their own heads by members of that body, so renowned for its durability, on which most of them had sat for decades. Mr. MacDougall, a practising surgeon, is therefore seen at present more as a floor-of-the-house member than as an establishment figure and is, in fact, a man from the outer world. This environment has not hitherto been strongly represented in Kennel Club upper echelons......."

It was said at the time that Mr MacDougall's appointment was as the result of clear recognition of the need for revitalisation — and revitalisation there was. In the next 15 years many things were to change but that change also brought Mr MacDougall his critics. There were many who likened his period in office, during which time he became not just chairman of the General Committee but chairman of the Kennel Club, to the period in office of Margaret Thatcher as Prime Minister.

She, too, had her detractors and both shared criticism of their style of government. John MacDougall once likened his role to that of an executive chairman of a company. Truly, he was, especially in those years after retirement from his surgeon's duties, spending more days at the Kennel Club than away from it. His mind encompassed every thing that was going on. He made sure the Kennel Club had friends in the Houses of Parliament and in every organisation which possibly could help the Kennel Club.

No General Committee member could ever attend a meeting without being fully cognisant of every sub-committee's work. To ask a question or make a statement without full knowledge or having read the minutes was asking to be whip-lashed by the sharp tongue of the chairman.

He oversaw a rewriting of the club's constitution and was a stickler for good sportsmanship at competitions. He represented the Kennel Club on the issue of quarantine which he believed eventually would be abolished. He helped to develop his wife's dream of a Kennel Club Junior Organisation, instigated the building and staffing of the Kennel Club library, he helped initiate the Good Citizen Dog Scheme. He established the Kennel Club Charitable Trust. It was under his chairmanship that Crufts moved from London to the National Exhibition Centre, Birmingham, where it has remained.

One remembers many other things accomplished by John MacDougall, things like the continuance of world kennel club congresses, begun by his predecessor, and his patronage of many dog-related activities.

He was not an easy man to know and yet he was a wonderful ambassador for Britain and its dogs. Gradually over the years, especially since his own retirement from work, a change came over the world of dogs which continues today.

67

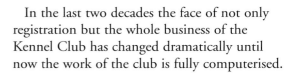

We see the Kennel Club slowly evolving to allow greater participation in the running of canine affairs by dogdom as a whole.

Not long before his death he successfully fought off a move by some members of the General Committee to remove him from office but by now he was a tired man.

When first he stood for General Committee, in 1979, he was not elected. The next year he was asked to stand again but, before allowing his name to go forward, he needed to know whether he stood any real chance of success. He did and his years in office are testimony to his worth.

Those who did not really know him are the poorer for that, for there was another side to John MacDougall which so many never saw. He was amusing to be with and he talked with interest and fun of his days as a young medical man. He had played rugby and loved cricket, but it was as the innovative and crusading chairman of the Kennel Club he will best be remembered.

J P C (PETER) JAMES

Chairman of the Kennel Club 1996-

*Peter James
Chairman of the Kennel
Club 1996-present*

Peter James is currently chairman of the Kennel Club but had a significant influence on the club long before his appointment to the chair. Although he had served as vice-chairman to John MacDougall, following in the place of Brig Alec Campbell, he was asked as long ago as 1979 by the then secretary of the Kennel Club to advise on the terms of the projected purchase of a computer system for registration of dogs.

Subsequently, independent consultants were engaged to help with the drawing up of a specification of requirements. This was put to tender and the resultant system installation served the Kennel Club until its more recent changes and the move of registrations to Aylesbury (see chapter on the homes of the Kennel Club).

In the last two decades the face of not only registration but the whole business of the Kennel Club has changed dramatically until now the work of the club is fully computerised.

Peter James' interest in computers dates back to his early life when, after education at All Saints School, Bloxham, Oxfordshire, and reading law at St Catherine's, Oxford, he set up his own company in the 1960s.

Many will remember his father, the late Jimmy James of Wendover Irish Setters and Labradors, who also served on the General Committee. Peter was born in 1931 in Northampton and came to the chair of the Kennel Club on the death of John MacDougall.

Since those tumultuous days when the bid to oust John MacDougall failed, Peter James has had a steadying influence on both the General Committee and the world of dogs. He may appear somewhat laid back in his approach to club matters but his grasp of what is going on is just as keen as that of his predecessor and it is still unwise to raise matters in General Committee without having prepared every bit as thoroughly as though John MacDougall were still presiding.

Peter James has a keen interest in the "grass roots" of dogdom and can be seen at both shows and field events. He has bred and shown show champion Irish Setters and enjoys the working side of dogs.

It was in 1981 that Peter James was invited to join the powerful Finance and General Purposes Committee, followed by election to the General Committee in 1983. He was elected vice chairman in 1987 and a Trustee of the Kennel Club just a year later.

Outside Kennel Club work he has served on the committee of the Irish Setter Association, England, since 1984 and was elected its president in 1996, a position he later relinquished when elected chairman of the Kennel Club. With his wife, Julie, he lives in the house at Gayton, Northamptonshire, formerly occupied by his parents. His vice-chairman is Peter Mann from Edinburgh, a member of the Kennel Club since 1980.

Valerie Foss and Bernard Hall

Not until 1979 were ladies full members

FOR 80 years the Kennel Club had a Ladies' Branch which flourished until the final admission of women into full membership of the club in 1979. The idea was mooted first in a letter received by the General Committee on September 8, 1896, from Lady Auckland. She suggested facilities should be offered to women to become members of the Kennel Club and a sub-committee appointed to consider the formation of a Ladies' Branch recommended this should happen. The recommendation was not agreed to by the General Committee.

At a special general meeting on February 9, 1899, Mr Francis Redmond proposed that a Ladies' Branch be formed. This was seconded by Mr J. H. Salter and the proposal met with general approval, there being only one dissentient, Mr S. J. Thompson, who proposed an amendment which failed to find a seconder.

It was decided the branch be formed immediately and its first committee be appointed by the committee of the Kennel Club. On July 4, that year, the names of 50 ladies were approved as the first members of the branch. Fifteen were chosen to serve on the branch committee and at its first meeting on July 19, 1899, the Duchess of Newcastle was elected to the chair with Mrs Sidney Turner her vice-chairman. The following ladies chaired the branch until women achieved the right to become full members of the Kennel Club:

The Duchess of Newcastle
1899 – 1901

The influence of the Duchess in the canine history of this time must never be underestimated. In breeding and showing her kennels ranked with the best and that a lady of her social eminence was so involved in the world of dogs caused other ladies to become interested. Before her marriage to the Duke, Kathleen Florence May Candy was the daughter of Major Henry Candy of the 9th Lancers, and the Hon Mrs Candy, daughter of the 3rd Baron Rossmore. Kathleen Candy married Henry Pelham Archibald Douglas Pelham-Clinton, 7th Duke of Newcastle, in 1889. The family addresses were Clumber Park, Worksop, (the 4th Duke was the 'Clumber Spaniel' Duke), Forest Farm, Windsor Forest (The Duchess' address in her later years of showing when the Duke was dead) and 11 Berkeley House, Hay Hill, W.1 The Duke and Duchess had no children so, upon his death the title went to his brother and became extinct in 1988 with the death of the 9th Duke who had no male heirs.

The Duchess of Newcastle with a Borzoi and a Smooth Fox Terrier. Chairman of the Ladies Branch of the Kennel Club 1899-1901

It seems that the Duchess first came across the Borzoi when her mother was given a dog called Spain, so called because he was given by a Spanish grandee, the Marquis of Quandelmina. She built up an important kennel of the breed from the 1890s, just after the breed had been fully recognised by the Kennel Club. She had sufficient money at her disposal to buy stock, and as there was no quarantine it was easier to import than it is today. The last Borzoi to be imported before the quarantine started was her Ch. Tsaretsa.

There was more contact between Britain and Russia than probably at any time because Tsar Nicholas II was the nephew of Queen Alexandra, as his mother, Princess Dagmar, was her sister. The Tsar had a kennel of Borzois at Gatchina, his hunting park, and some of these were brought over to be exhibited at the leading British shows. Sixteen were shown at Crufts in 1892, but from a picture it can be seen they were mostly very badly constructed. However the Duchess purchased Oudar, the best of the lot, reputedly for £200.

The Duchess bred eight Borzoi champions and owned another five. She owned the first bitch champion, the Russian-bred Ch. Milka, and bred the first British bitch champion Ch. Vikhra. Her stud dogs were influential just at the point where the breed was becoming established in this country. Ch. Velsk was the sire of five champions, including three in one litter, to Ch. Tsaretsa. Ch. Vikhra was also the dam of three champions. The Duchess' top winning Borzoi was Ch. Tsaretsa with 17 CCs, the breed record until just before the First World War.

In the chapter on the paintings and trophies of the Kennel Club there is much about the Duchess. With her Ch. Podar of Notts she had one of the most influential Borzois of all time and virtually all of today's hounds are traced back in tail male to him. The Duchess bred 12 Wire Fox Terrier champions between 1900 and 1923. The first was the influential Ch. Cackler of Notts, considered to be the ancestor of every Wire Fox Terrier in the world. The last champion the Duchess bred was a Smooth Fox Terrier, Ch. Correct Wartax of Notts. She bred nine Smooth Fox Terrier champions and bought in another two. A keen student of breeding, the Duchess line-bred using stud dogs from Mrs Losco Bradley's Cromwell Kennel which traced back to Francis Redmond's great rival, Mr. Vicary. On the death of the Duchess in 1955 (the Duke had died in 1928) she left to the Kennel Club pictures and cups. She left her show dogs to her kennel man. To her maid was left the choice of the Duchess' house dogs, all the other house dogs, as soon as possible, to be put down for she was worried that they could end up neglected or uncared for. She was a well known judge of her breeds.

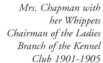

Mrs. Chapman with her Whippets Chairman of the Ladies Branch of the Kennel Club 1901-1905

Mrs Charles Chapman
1901-1905

Mrs Chapman was formerly Mrs Oughton-Giles and was well known as an exhibitor of pocket Beagles and Whippets. She is included with these two breeds in the well known book *'Dog Shows and Doggy People'*. Writing about the Ladies' Branch in his history of the Kennel Club Jaquet mentions that as Mrs Chapman she also showed Bloodhounds.

Mrs. Oliphant
Chairman of the Ladies Branch of the Kennel Club 1905-1915

Mrs. E. K. Oliphant
1905-1915

Mrs Oliphant's affix was Chatley, under which she bred Bloodhounds. There were five champions which carried the kennel name, Ch Chatley Brilliant and Ch Chatley Blazer, made up in 1903, Ch Chatley Beaufort in 1906, Ch Chatley Harebell, in 1909 and the last Crufts triple winner, Ch Chatley Truelass in 1931. It is still possible to see Blazer today as he has been preserved and is on show at the Natural History Museum at Tring.

John Emms painted Blazer trailing a scent and he is mounted at Tring in the same position as in his portrait. His sister, Brilliant, is also at Tring but not on display, Truelass was sold to Mrs Elms of the Reynalton affix and she was one of the only two people owning Bloodhounds which could be bred from after the Second World War.

Mrs Gwendoline Powys Romilly
1915-1922

Mrs Romilly had been vice-chairman to Mrs Oliphant and on her resignation became chairman in 1915. Mrs Romilly's dog involvement was jointly with her husband, Col.

Mrs. Romilly with Ch.Ambroise and Ch.André
Chairman of the Ladies Branch of the Kennel Club 1915-1922

F. W. Romilly, CVO CO DSO, who became a member of the General Committee of the Kennel Club in 1912 and a vice-president in 1933. Their prefix was Taplow and their breed French Bulldogs, in which they had many champions. They first became involved as early as 1894 and took one to India in 1896 where Col Romilly was Military Secretary to the Governor of Madras. Mrs Romilly was one of the first honorary treasurers of the French Bulldog Club of England and later became president. Mrs Romilly, who also judged the breed, died on December 20, 1936, just over a year later than her husband.

Lorna Countess Howe
1922-1948

It was as Mrs Quentin Dick, wife of Capt. Quentin Dick, a famous sportsman, that she became chairman of the Ladies' Branch. Her husband died in 1923 and four years later she became the third wife of the 4th Earl Howe. She was the daughter of Major Ernest Charles Penn Curzon and one of the most important men or women of her era in dogs. When the Labrador Retriever Club was started in 1916 she became the first secretary and treasurer, remaining in these offices until her death in 1961. She became the second chairman in 1935, another office she held until her death.

It is widely believed that the present popularity of the Labrador was due mainly to her work, as she started in the breed just five years after the first champion had been made up. She was determined that the breed was to remain dual purpose, and owned four of the ten dual purpose champions ever made up. In the 1923 Club Yearbook she wrote;

"Happily the majority of dogs that have won a CC have qualified in the field. It is sincerely to be hoped that such a state will long continue and that Labradors may, for many years to come, have representatives of the breed that compete successfully not only in their own classes but in classes open to all varieties and show that working gun dogs should be so high in quality and symmetrical in shape that they can hold their own amongst the best show dogs of the day."

But, unfortunately, once the Countess died and she could no longer influence breeders, the breed split into the lighter, maybe over-speedy working dog and the heavy maybe over-ponderous show specimen. She knew that this was going to happen when she was no longer able to influence the progress of the breed.

Her first Labrador was Scandal of Glynn and he was the sire of Banchory Bolo (bred by Major H. Banner) the first dual champion in the breed. Scandal was one of her favourite dogs, sleeping in a basket in her room, and his mistress always said that she learnt more from him than he did from her. When he died it was years before the Countess could bear to have another personal dog. Scandal had sired only one litter because of the restrictions on breeding brought about by the First World War and from this set of puppies, born in 1915, there was only one dog puppy, Bolo. The litter was now three years old and it took a while for the Countess' husband to track him down, but by this time he was a wayward and surly dog who was considered untrainable. It took much hard work for the Countess to gain his trust and train him to field trial standard and his field trial title.

Lorna Countess Howe
Chairman of the Ladies
Branch of the Kennel
Club 1922-1948

Her trainer and handler was Mr Thomas Gaunt, who managed the kennel for over 30 years. He was also a respected field trial judge, dying in 1963 aged 84.

The Countess bred only two champions. All the other 26, were bought in. Apparently if a dog was placed above the one that the Countess was exhibiting she would look it over as she stood further down the line, and if she agreed with the dog's placing she would try to buy it there and then, before they had left the ring.

In 1932 another dual champion was made up, his name Bramshaw Bob. At Crufts Bob won all his six classes, the dog CC, best of breed and best in show. Crufts in these days was a great meeting place for gamekeepers and this was a most popular win. Frank Warner Hill wrote 'Didn't the gun dog folk and the many keepers present give owner and dog an ovation. They appreciated such a great win with a proved working dog.'

Bob returned to Crufts the next year and repeated his previous win of BIS. In all he won 13 championship BIS titles.

After the war the first post-war champion was her Ch Orchardton Du O'Banchory. She had two final champions, Ch Banchory Cottager in 1948 and Ch British Justice in 1950. Justice won 21 CCs before his early death at five years. He ran well at field trials and the Countess said of him that he was the true type of Labrador with a charming disposition and character. Countess Howe also had champion pugs. She judged at trials and shows and was co-opted to sit on the Kennel Club's field trial committee.

Miss Marion Keyte-Perry
1948-1963

Miss Keyte-Perry had ten Samoyed champions in the years before the Second World War. Her prefix was Arctic and one can still see them in a marvellous photograph taken by Thomas Fall. Miss Keyte-Perry was a headmistress at a private boarding school for girls at Oak Hall, Haslemere, Surrey. The pupils were allowed to groom the dogs and the Arctic spitz breeds seem to have been part of

Miss Marion Keyte Perry (on the left), with Miss H. Voy at a Kennel Club banquet, 1958. Keyte Perry was Chairman of the Ladies Branch of the Kennel Club 1948-1963

the curriculum. She was an interesting, complex and at times amusing character.

In the words of her vice-chairman of the Ladies' Branch, Clara Bowring, "I had a great personal admiration for her splendid qualities of both heart and brain. She had such a sanity of outlook and such integrity of mind and heart, a great schoolmistress and a great dog breeder".

Miss Keyte-Perry judged a number of breeds and best in show at championship shows. She was first chairman and then president of the British Samoyed Club for well over 30 years. She was the author of *The Samoyed, Survey from Ancient History to the Present Day.* She resigned as Ladies' Branch chairman in 1963 and died in February 1967.

Mrs Lumsden and Miss Clara Bowring (on the right) Clara Bowring was Chairman of the Ladies Branch of the Kennel Club 1963-1969

Miss Clara Bowring
1963-1969

There are still people living today who knew the last four chairmen of the Ladies' Branch and Miss Clara Bowring has been described as a kind and considerate friend to many but, if she did not like you, heaven help you!

Her breed was Shetland Sheepdogs and she showed in partnership with her cousin, Mrs. Lumsden of Clova. Larkbeare was their prefix and Ch. Larkbeare Rusk was either the third or fourth dog champion to be made up. Mr. Lumsden of Clova was one of the first people to bring Shelties from the Islands to the mainland and he played a large part in getting them recognised by the Kennel Club. In 1929 Miss Bowring became secretary of the English Shetland Sheepdog Club and from 1948 to 1961 its chairman.

Clara Bowring was also very involved with Poodles and the colour which most interested her was blue, that most difficult colour to breed. She was president of the Poodle Club and wrote in conjunction with Alida Munro, the Popular Dogs book on *The Poodle* which is still very readable today. During the Second World War she worked for the Land Army and was stationed at Henley-on-Thames.

She was an excellent chairman of the Ladies' Branch and had the art of keeping people to the point. She always kept her temper and could see both sides of a question. She judged her breeds and was a judge people liked to watch.

Dr. E. M. Frankling and Mr. Gerald Austin. Dr. Frankling was Chairman of the Ladies Branch of the Kennel Club 1969-1971

Dr. Eleanor M. Frankling
1969-1971

Dr. Frankling MA (Cantab), LRCP, MRCS, joined the Ladies' Branch of the Kennel Club in 1948 and after serving as vice-chairman succeeded Miss Clara Bowring as chairman on September 15, 1969. Her main canine interest was Dalmatians and her prefix Winnall. She bred Ch. Winnall Blackberry, exhibited Ch. Elegance and Ch. Winnall Dazzler of Dalmally and Ch. Winnall Bearscombe Betony. She gave great help to the Dutch Dalmatian breeders after the Second World War and the puppies she sent to them were almost a new foundation of the breed in Holland.

As a canine author she was world famous. Her *Practical Dog Breeding and Genetics* is as relevant now as when published in 1961. Her book on *The Dalmatian* in the Popular Dogs series is another that has stood the test of time. Her appointment in 1967 to serve on the special sub-committee set up under the chairmanship of Sir Dudley Forwood to consider the position of cryptorchids, was an important step in the equality of women within the Kennel club.

Ill health forced her to retire from the chairmanship and she died in January, 1975.

Mrs. Yvonne Bentinck
1971-1979

"Eve" Bentinck was the daughter of Col. and Mrs. Harold Street, who married W.B. Bentinck, son of Admiral Sir Rudolph and Lady Bentinck. Her first dog was a Cocker Spaniel, acquired in the Twenties. She later turned her attentions to Deerhounds in which she won her first C.C.

Having moved to Devon in 1947, she bred her first litter of Pekingese in 1949 and it was in this breed that her Copplestone prefix was to achieve world fame. Her first champion was Int. Ch. Copplestone Pai-Phu who gained his title in 1956 and while there were many champions, her best known was undoubtedly Int. Ch. Copplestone Pu Zin, a group and best in show winner at championship level.

Mrs. Bentinck (left) with Mrs. Nagle and Miss Surrell Mrs. Bentinck was Chairman of the Ladies Branch of the Kennel Club 1971-1979

Exports from the Copplestone kennel were numerous and two of the last were exquisite miniatures, Copplestone Mr and Miss Pinkcoat, who went to the States.

In 1969 tragedy struck Mrs. Bentinck when a fire wiped out her kennel. Having lost her kennel, Mrs. Bentinck resolved to concentrate on the judging career which she had started in 1950 and she soon became a championship show judge of many toy breeds, later adding several breeds in other groups. She was a judge at best in show level and had undertaken many overseas judging trips. She became a member of the Ladies' Branch of the Kennel Club in 1940, its vice-chairman in 1969 and at the time of its amalgamation with the Kennel Club proper, was its chairman.

She was a tireless worker. Both the Invicta Pekingese Club and the Sleeve Dog Club (which she reactivated) owed her a great debt. At the time of her death on July 16, 1986, she was an active committee member of the West of England Ladies' Kennel Society, The Ladies' Kennel Association and East of England championship show committees

Valerie Foss.

F Muller. This painting of an officer with his dogs and horse is signed F. Muller. On the back of the canvas, which has a 20th century relining, has been inked 'Painted by Duke Alexander of Wurttemberg.' It is possible that the picture was painted by Franz Xaver Muller, who was born at the end of the 18th century, especially as he was painter at the court of Wurttemberg, and that the painting is of, rather than by, Duke Alexander. Bears signature and date, oil on canvas, 15¹/₂ x 12".

Geoffrey Davien, Sculpt.
Cold cast resin bronze model by Heredities Ltd.
of the German Shepherd Dog, Ramacon Swashbuckler,
commemorating the dog's Best in Show at Crufts in 1971.
This is number 1 of an edition of 350. 10¹/₂" high.

Stud Books, Calendar and Gazette

*O*NE *of the reasons* for the foundation of the Kennel Club was the need for a stud book, which leads automatically into the situation that whoever owned the Stud Book and thus, by definition, the right to enter dogs into the same Stud Book was a long way into becoming the supreme judicature and controlling body of the emerging dog world.

Read the following quotation from E.W. Jaquet's *History of the Kennel Club*. "One of the earliest undertakings of the newly-formed Kennel Club was the compilation of a Stud Book. In preparing the book, Mr S. E. Shirley, founder of the Kennel Club, consulted Mr Walsh – at that time editor of *The Field.* Mr Walsh strongly recommended Mr Frank C. S. Pearce as the editor and that gentleman, having been selected, at once set to work, the first volume of the Kennel Club Stud Book being ready for distribution at the Birmingham Show, held on December 1st and the three following days, 1874.

"Mr. Frank C.S. Pearce was the son of the Rev. Thomas Pearce, the well known 'Idstone' of *The Field.* The volume contains over 600 pages and is in every respect a most admirable production."

The first volume covered from 1859-1874 and in Frank Pearce's own words, "This work, prepared by me for the Kennel Club, has been produced at a great and necessary expense, and is intended to fill up a blank in the history of the canine world. The lapse of many years since the first show has made it difficult to obtain reliable information, and has caused much delay, more attributable to the owners of the dogs than to the compiler. As the work is of so novel a nature, I have found no precedent to guide me in its preparation, but I commenced it only after discussing the subject with the best authorities of the day. By rigidly excluding or pointing out all doubtful pedigrees, I have endeavoured to make it as much a record of fact and truth as possible and if it be incomplete,

I can only say that it must be borne in mind that a dog unlike a horse, may have several lots of offspring in the year, and brings in some instance as many as 15 or 20 puppies into the world at a time, and that I have applied for pedigrees to at least 3,500 persons."

The volume contains the pedigrees of 4,027 dogs divided into 40 classes, and considering the difficulties of attending the preparation of a work of such magnitude is remarkably accurate. Published in the first volume of the *Stud Book* is the Code of Rules for the guidance of Dog Shows, and also those for the guidance of Field Trials of Sporting Dogs, framed by the Kennel Club in 1874.

The Kennel Club Stud Books, from the first edition in 1874, to the present day. The Kennel Club Yearbook became a separate publication in 1966.

Jaquet mentions that both codes have a most archaic appearance in the light of latter day legislation. Nowadays of course, rules and regulations are all in the *Kennel Club Year Book,* another famous 'red book', for the binding of the Stud Books has been in the main in different shades of red. To date there are 126 volumes in all, remembering the first volume covered 1859-1874, a period of 15 years. It was published from *The Field* office with pages 1-7 filled with advertisements. In the preface Frank Pearce thanks the many members of the aristocracy, starting with the Prince of Wales, who had helped him and included are the names many of the great sporting men whose kennels are written into the early history of many breeds such as The Duke of Buccleuch (Labradors), Sir Vincent Corbet (Setters), Sir Watkin Wynne (many gundogs), S.E. Shirley (gundogs, terriers), Mr. Lloyd Price (many gundogs), Mr. Purcell Llewellin (English Setters), Rev. J.C. Macdona (St. Bernards),

Rev. T. Pearce (Idstone), J.H. Walsh (Stonehenge) and J.H. Salter, (the latter three being famous authors and judges), Mr R. Garth (Pointers), Mr. E. Laverack (English Setters) and Mr. W. Lort (a famous judge).

He also mentions that Mr. Shirley saw all the proofs and had almost as much trouble throughout as he did himself. The contents page of this first book which had more pages of information than any till we reach the 13th K.C. Stud Book gives us the rules of the Kennel Club.

Some interesting facts emerge: Not more than 100 members, exclusive of all honorary members; the candidates for membership must give their name, rank, residence and profession or occupation – if any; entrance fee five guineas, annual subscription five guineas; committee of 15 members; annual general meeting held in Birmingham, if possible during the week of the annual exhibition; no member of the club shall under any circumstances knowingly either enter or exhibit a dog or dogs, at any competition under a false name, age, pedigree, breeder or description.

Mr. Carberry, Col. H. M. Wilson, F. C. Lowe, Francis Redmond, and Major Kelly These men's achievements filled many pages of the Stud Book.

The list of members, with H.R.H. the Prince of Wales as patron comprised great sporting men of their time. Ladies were not admitted. There were quite a few members of the aristocracy – Marquis of Buchanan, the Hon. R.C. Hill, later Viscount Hill, Marquis of Huntley, who served on the committee, the Hon. Gerald Lascelles later Lord Harewood and the Earl of Onslow. Of the 51 members there were judges and exhibitors who were responsible

for forming the dog world of yesterday, namely Major Allison Daintry Hollins, George Brewis, William Lort, Rev. J.C. Macdona, J.R. Murchison, R.J.L. Price, S.E. Shirley and J.H. Walsh.

The Code of Rules, ten in number, addressed the problems of the time and it is interesting to see how the rules have changed over the years as the dog world has changed. There was also a Code of 11 rules for the Guidance of Field Trials of Sporting Dogs and a scale of points for judging field trials of pointers and setters, having been suggested by several gentlemen.

Then came the shows, starting with the first at Newcastle in 1859. The second was held also in 1859 at Birmingham and all classes had the name of the owners of the winners. Then follow 1860, Birmingham; 1861, Leeds; 1861, Manchester; 1862, Agricultural Hall, London. The list continues up to 1873 – the 13th show for Manchester.

The first field trial was April 18th 1865, on the ground of Mr. S. Whitebread, MP, at Southill, Bedfordshire. In the *Stud Book,* we can read the exact description of the ground, scenting conditions and the correspondence that the trial occasioned. The trials reports continue until the final one of 1873 which was the Kennel Club's own held at Ipswich where one of the judges was S.E. Shirley himself.

The next section is the groups, breeds and pedigrees. A whole page is taken up for Mr. Edwin Brough's Bloodhound dog Rufus. There are 13 pages for Fox Terrier dogs, 11 pages for Fox Terrier bitches. One of the problems for the early compilers of the *Stud Book,* was the multiplicity of the same name; five Violet's in Wire Fox Terrier bitches, 14 Bangs in Pointer dogs. Edward Laverack's English Setters are supported by a full pedigree table and it is interesting to see what pedigree researchers have become used to with old pedigrees – the name of the owner as well as the dog, for example Mr Garth's Bess by Mr. Fawkes' Rap (Edmund Castle breed) out of Mr. Forrester's Fan. The final breed Toy Terriers (roughs and broken haired) shows that of the 46 dogs entered only two exhibitors did not come from the North of England.

Vol. II of the *Stud Book* was a much slimmer version in green binding, this being one of the few exceptions from variations of red. Again it was compiled and edited by Frank Pearce, at the request of the Kennel Club and published for the Kennel Club at the *Field* office in The Strand. Before starting Vol. VII Mr. Pearce asked for suggestions from breeders and exhibitors and the answers received were carefully considered and often used. It contains 12 championship shows and three field trials but at this stage the whole description of the trial was written up. Dogs then were not divided into the groups of today, just into sporting and non-sporting. This continued until 1884 when the divisions were dropped, but they were reintroduced in 1902.

There was a problem with the Birmingham Dog Show Society whose members thought it advisable that they should publish a stud book of their own realising that, if they did not, the Kennel Club would become the paramount authority. Arrangements for the Birmingham stud book started, but they soon hit the first obstacle. They thought they could use the Kennel Club's reference numbers, but Mr. Shirley as joint owner of the copyright prevented the infringement. So Birmingham did not go ahead with its own stud book and a later meeting soothed the problems between the two bodies and one outcome was that Birmingham Dog Show Society became entitled to send two gentlemen to represent the society on the committee of the Kennel Club.

With the publication of the third volume of the *Stud Book* Frank Pearce states the problem of giving ancestors for every dog and for the retrievers, collies and toys to be given even the sire and dam, was often impossible. He thought the only way to overcome this was that the committees of shows insist on pedigrees, if known, being supplied by every exhibitor, suggesting that if this rule were adopted and enforced the canine *Stud Book* would resemble and be as important as the *Herd Book* and *Equine Stud Book*. Although the *Stud Book* for the time was still published by the *Field* the preface, written by Frank Pearce, gave as the address the first home of the Kennel Club at 2 Albert Mansions, Victoria St, London.

By Volume IV covering the year 1876 the Kennel Club had moved to larger premises 29a Pall Mall, London, S.W. The *Stud Book* was no longer compiled by Frank Pearce, but must have become the work of the first Kennel Club secretary, George Lowe. The books continued in the same format, informing the members what had happened over the year, of club rules, the committee of the Kennel Club, list of members, rules for dog shows and field trials, list of the dog shows, with venue, judges and prize list and then the pedigrees of the dogs entered.

By 1880 the new rules came into force regarding registrations. In his book *The Kennel Club, a History and Record of Its Work*, Edward Jaquet says 'For the most part the press of that day with a singular lack of foresight and discernment, failed utterly to recognise the principle involved. It was quite willing to acknowledge the great advancement and improvement in the status of the dog brought about by the Kennel Club but chafed under the additional regulations which that body found it necessary to add to the code if good government was to be maintained.'

It was ever thus, as the same criticism has followed the legislature of the Kennel Club to the present day. Registration meant that a permanent record is established by means of which the dog registered may be identified. We do not meet so many dogs registered with humorous names nowadays but in the late 1870s a well known supporter of field trials tendered the following names which were accepted for registration: John the Baptist, Joseph in Egypt and Abraham's Wife. Once seen in the *Kennel Gazette* the clerical members of the club were much perturbed, so the owner was asked to change the names which, in the next *Kennel Gazette* he did, the registration for the three English Setters being amended to Our Jack, Our Joe and Our Sal!

The *Kennel Gazette* was founded originally by Mr. Shirley and, although intimately connected with the club, it was the private property of its founder. While it contained much official matter it was not the Kennel Club's official organ. At the committee meeting held at the Alexandra Palace on January 19th 1881, Mr. Shirley referred to the success it had attained and that the general opinion of the members of the club was that the *Kennel Gazette* should belong to the club as its official organ, and therefore he handed it over. Mr Lowe, who had been associated with him in the journal, wished to devote himself entirely to duties in connection with the *Kennel Gazette* and for that purpose wished to resign the duties of the secretaryship. Mr F. Wilson was appointed secretary in his place.

77

By the tenth volume there was far greater accuracy in the *Stud Book* and those who had knowledge of the breeds were asked to check the pedigrees and, as most were 'founding fathers' of their breeds, it must have helped greatly for pedigree accuracy. By now Henry St James Stephen, a barrister, was secretary, a post he held until 1885.

The *Stud Book* was now showing an increase in the club rules from the original 16 to 32, with the majority defining the powers and duties of the committee. It was decided to hold regular meetings on the first Tuesday of every month. Before that meetings had been held whenever business demanded. The volume for 1883 records the formation of a body of associates, a body of ladies and gentlemen interested in canine matters. The first election saw 52 approved and their names published in the *Kennel Gazette* and then in the *Stud Book*. One important aspect of the associates was ladies being allowed membership from the beginning. This year, 1883, also saw the Kennel Club move to 6 Cleveland Row and the election of the first House Committee. In 1899 a special general meeting was held at the Club House, then at Old Burlington Street, when Mr. Francis Redmond proposed, seconded by Mr J.H. Salter, the formation of a Ladies Branch of the Kennel Club. The only dissenting voice was that of Mr S. J. Thompson. The motion was carried and it was decided that the first committee should be appointed by the committee of the Kennel Club. This was also the year Mr S.E. Shirley resigned the chairmanship of the Kennel Club committee. He was later made president after the club rules were amended. In 1901 the *Stud Book* reported that Edward W Jaquet had become secretary of the Kennel Club, a post he filled for 20 more years.

With the passing years the Kennel Club *Stud Book* took on very much the size and appearance of today's works. The 1914 book provided information about the effect of the war, postponement of the Kennel Club's 59th championship show among other things. The volumes for the years 1917,1918-1919 were very slim editions as there were few championship shows held, just six in 1917 none for 1918 and, two in 1919, but the club decided it would be undesirable that the sequence of the *Kennel Club Calendar and Stud Book* should be suspended. The Kennel Club address was now 84 Piccadilly, London. W.1.

The following direct quotation about not keeping large kennels during the war explains how many of the larger kennels were lost, never to return.

"On May 14 a deputation from the Committee of the Club, consisting of Mr. J. Sidney Turner (Chairman) Mr. Mark Beaufoy, Mr. Walter S. Glynn, Mr. Francis Redmond, and Mr E. W. Jaquet (Secretary) was received at the Treasury, on behalf of the Chancellor of the Exchequer, by Mr. Stanley Baldwin M.P. The Chairman, in introducing the deputation, called attention to the widespread concern, which had been aroused by the statement of the Chancellor when placing his proposals before the House of Commons, as to a suggested increase on the present tax on dogs. He pointed out the attitude of the Kennel Club upon the various other questions involved, and, further, referred to the necessity of stringently enforcing the regulations of the existing Dogs' Act as it affects stray and useless dogs. Mr. Stanley Baldwin gave the deputation a very sympathetic hearing, and in thanking the members for their attendance especially expressed his obligation for the assurance given him of their desire to render Government every assistance in their power which might help in the consideration of the questions at issue.

On July 19 Mr. Bonar Law, the Chancellor of the Exchequer, made a statement to the House of Commons, in the course of which he announced that orders had been issued under the Defence of the Realm Act strengthening the administrative machinery in respect of stray dogs and prohibiting dog shows, and proceeded as follows:

'The Food Controller has been in constant communication with the various associations of breeders and other people interested in dogs, and has found them ready to fall in with his views and effect economies in the food supply. He has informed me that the steps taken by the Kennel Club, supplemented by the voluntary actions of the breeders, has resulted in a considerable reduction in kennels; that this reduction is increasing, and that after September 8 no puppies will be registered by the Club, for the period of the War, except those bred under special licence from the Club; and that foxhounds have been reduced voluntarily by 40-50%. I hope that in view of the action taken by the Government and the voluntary response by dog owners generally, it will not prove necessary to resort to increased taxation, and, as at present advised, it is not my intention to propose it.'

On June 27 the Committee had under consideration the Government's desire to save food fit for human consumption, which might otherwise be used as food for puppies, and it was decided that on and after September 8, for the period of the War, no puppies born shall be registered except such as are from litters bred under the licence of the Kennel Club. At their meeting on July 11, the Committee decided that following the above resolution an appeal be made to breeders to abstain from breeding the puppies for the period specified, and notified the Kennel Club cannot guarantee after the War the registration of any puppies bred in contravention of these resolutions. From the date of these resolutions the Committee had been in constant communication with the Government in regard to the restrictions on breeding.

On October 25, a letter was received from the Ministry of Food setting forth in unmistakable terms that the Government was unable, at present, to accede to any application to relax their regulation, and that the Chancellor of the Exchequer had directed the Minister of Food to inform the Kennel Club that he should view with disfavour any relaxation of the regulations with regard to breeding and the reduction of stock, and to intimate that unless there is a reduction of breeding it might lead to a re-opening of the subject of taxation. In view of this communication the Committee at a special meeting held on November 28 decided that no further breeding licences will for the present be issued.

Following the announcement by the Government that dog shows were altogether prohibited, the attention of the General Committee has been continually directed to the question of the re-instatement of radius shows."

In the late 1800s the *Stud Book* started to carry the lists of prefixes and affixes and by 1923 was back to its previous size. Edward Jaquet, one of the greatest of the Kennel Club's secretaries, died in 1921 and now H.T.W. Bowell was secretary, a position he filled for 18 years. As rules were changed or added to, they appeared in the *Kennel Gazette* and then finally in the *Stud Book* for the year they had been passed. The *Stud Book* of 1933 was a format that continued for many years, with its contents including committee and sub-committee details, summary of events for the year, championship shows, open, limited and sanction shows, lists of matches, Scottish Kennel Club sanction shows, list of classified breeds and breed statistics, registrations, Kennel Club rules, show regulations, regulations as to the preparation of dogs for exhibition, and for the definitions of classes at open and limited shows.

Further pages dealt with instructions to show secretaries, field trial and working trial rules, lists of members, Ladies Branch members, Associate members, lists of breed societies, general canine societies, affiliated colonial clubs, clubs with reciprocal agreements, prefixes and affixes, lists of winners of challenge certificates, shows, field trials, working trials, list of Kennel Club challenge cups and trophies, names and addresses of people whose dogs are entered in the volume and finally, advertisements.

The book for 1939 showed King George VI as patron. The president was HRH the Duke of Connaught and Strathearn. Vice Presidents included two more Dukes, Atholl and Hamilton, Earl Lonsdale, Viscount Powerscourt, W.L. McCandlish, no longer chairman but now also representing Birmingham Dog Show Society. The chairman of the committee was A. Croxton Smith. The introduction tells us that following the declaration of war on September 3, 1939 the activities of the dog world were severely curtailed and all the remaining championship shows for the year were abandoned. In the *Setter and Pointer Club Year Book* of 1946 an article by the famous judge Lola MacDonald Daly describes what it was like in those days: *"The last championship show we knew was Harrogate Sept. 2, 1939. The blackout had come upon us for the first time the night before and the lights of dogdom were going out as the figurative lights of bigger things were going out all over Europe. We talked in undertones, we thought of old so and so*

who has already decided to shoot all his dogs, we took our prize cards rather guiltily, because we had managed to get through while perhaps our strongest rival had gone off to join his regiment."

So Harrogate was the last championship show to be held until after the war. A further addition in the *Stud Book* was a complete list of dogs who had obtained their junior warrants since the introduction of the award in January, 1938, a total of 112 dogs. The next five books, 1942-1946, represented war years and were slim but again, as in the first war, the books were published so as not to spoil the sequence. Valuable records were sent to the country home of F.N. Pickett, a member of the General Committee, and some more records were stored in the country at the home of J.V. Rank, a trustee of the KC. Some of the more important pictures were taken to their homes by W.L. McCandlish, vice president of the club and Captain T.H. Hudson, member of the committee. With the end of the war in 1945 there was the return of the championship shows held by the specialist clubs. The Setter and Pointer Club held the only championship shows for English, Irish and Gordon Setters and Pointers at the Winter Gardens, Blackpool. The secretary was Harold Roberts, a member of the General Committee and later famous as secretary of Blackpool Championship Show. Lola MacDonald Daly now wrote *"But Blackpool! it was as if everyone who had ever owned a half leg interest in a Setter or Pointer had made up his mind to play a part in making this a renaissance which would be unforgettable. The reunion was tremendous; its spirit such that the results almost became secondary. Any of us who feared that the acrimony of the sanction show (an acrimony that, I suppose, must always exist where first prizes are cheap and bad dogs can win) might persist, since sanction shows were all that wartime had given us, and affect even the well remembered atmosphere of a big show, soon had their fears removed."*

Stonethorpe Stunner progressed through his three classes to win the first post war Pointer certificate. Stunner's owner Jim Davies was a Welshman and as Stunner won the CC Welshmen yelled and jumped as if at Twickenham.

The feature of the show was the success of the 'new brigade', many attending their first championship show. Mr W. Foss, late husband of Mrs Val Foss, wartime newcomer to English

Setters and with experience confined to Midland radius shows, exhibited Rombalds Revel. Not only did he win the dog CC but also the reserve C.C. in bitches with the latter titled Sh. Ch. Pamina of Ketree. The *Stud Book* shows an increasing number of shows with Alsatians (German Shepherd Dogs) as they were then called, having six sets of CCs. It was still the golden days of smooth and wire Fox Terriers with ten sets of CCs each. The *Stud Book* continued in the same format, Vol LXXXVI (1959) amended rule 4, that is championship shows to include the title Show Champion. The sub-committees were now very much as at the present day. As well as the field trials committee there was a working trials and obedience committee. The books were increasing in size. Certain modifications had been made in the past to reduce it to reasonable proportions, one of which was the contraction of pedigrees to two generations only instead of three.

During 1964 the committee set out the pedigree section in a different way which once again allowed pedigrees to be extended to three generations. Also commencing with the 1966 issue two volumes were to be published, one to be called the *Kennel Club Year Book* and contain Kennel Club Rules and Regulations in addition to items previously published in the beginning of the *Stud Book*. So the birth of the Red Book was accomplished and, of course, has become an integral part of the Kennel Club's publishing list. In the 1988 volume (No CXXV) are listed the ten sub-committees which report to the General Committee.

What would Frank Field, compiler of those first Kennel Club stud books think of these numbers for 1998? – Hound group, 34 breeds and 11,599 registrations; Terrier group, 26 breeds, 40,222 registrations; Utility group, 25 breeds, 25,346 registrations; Working and Pastoral, 51 breeds together, 60585 registrations; Toy group, 23 breeds, 31,538 registrations; Gundog group, 31 breeds and 89,656 registrations.

Qualifications for entry in the *Stud Book* are set out in the "K" regulations of the annual *Year Book*.

Here is how the *Stud Book* is compiled today: details of all dogs and bitches which have won *Stud Book* qualifying awards at championship shows and trials throughout the year; championship breed, obedience, working trial and field trial results are taken from the marked catalogues received from each of the above shows and entered by the awards department on to the computer. Only qualifying awards are computed and if a dog does not already have a *Stud Book* number, the computer will automatically generate one.

At the end of the year, once all the awards are on the computer, proofs of the *Stud Book* are printed. Each breed is sent to a checker for validation to ensure the accuracy of the information. At present 160 checkers are used and all donate their time voluntarily.

The checkers are given one month to return the proofs. Once a complete set of group proofs has been received and corrected the results are saved on to Microsoft Word and sent by e-mail to the printers, who produce the page format and send the information back to the Kennel Club office for final proof reading and approval.

More about the *Gazette*

In the early part of this chapter the *Kennel Gazette* was mentioned and how S.E. Shirley handed it over to the club in 1881. The *Gazette* has gone through many stages and those who read the early editions notice no punches were pulled and a lot of interesting information was either in articles or the letter pages. Research can solve puzzles even to-day. For example S.E. Shirley's Laverack English Setter Rogue K C S B 7172 died as the result of swallowing a cork. How odd one thinks but would never dream of finding out more except that …. the *Kennel Gazette* November, 1882, had the following paragraph in Club and Kennel Notes:

"During the last few months three very valuable dogs have died from precisely the same sort of mishap, namely, swallowing corks. Mr. Daintry Hollin's pure Laverack setter, had just been got in condition for the grouse season, when he was suddenly taken ill and died the next day. A few weeks ago Mr. Statter's Regent, by Champion Rock, and thought by those who had seen him to have been one of the most beautiful setters ever seen, was taken ill, and he died also within a few hours. In both these cases the dogs were opened, and in each a cork was found in the large intestines. Last Saturday **Bell's Life** *reported that Mr. O'Brien's greyhound Marston Moor, on the morning of the South of Ireland (Cork) Meeting, died so suddenly that his owner suspected foul play. On being opened, however, a large bottle cork was*

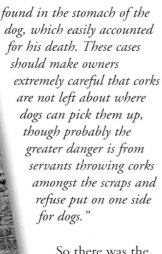

found in the stomach of the dog, which easily accounted for his death. These cases should make owners extremely careful that corks are not left about where dogs can pick them up, though probably the greater danger is from servants throwing corks amongst the scraps and refuse put on one side for dogs."

So there was the probable answer. The *Gazette* has gone through many guises but few people who read the *Kennel Gazette* in 1980 would recognise it as the same publication today. Before 1980 the *Gazette* was essentially a journal listing committee decisions, show dates and official communications. Over the years it has developed into a bright, colourful and vibrant publication constantly changing to meet the requirements and interests of its readership.

The modern *Kennel Gazette* started from somewhat utilitarian beginnings. There were no colour pages, few articles and the straightforward lists of information and events were rather dry to digest. As the success and professionalism of the Kennel Club itself grew so, too, did the need for a more polished magazine which

represents the Kennel Club to everyone involved in the canine world. January, 1984, saw the launch of a new look *Gazette* including in-depth articles on a wider variety of canine issues and a colour cover. These innovations were greeted with great enthusiasm by the readership and four years later, in October, 1988, the decision was taken to enhance the magazine still further to make it comparable with the sort of publication to be found on general sale on the news stands.

As well as a colourful, professionally designed cover, much greater use was made of photographs to illustrate the articles which covered a multitude of canine topics from canine health and behaviour to dogs in art, and included reports on the whole spectrum of canine events in this country and abroad. February 1989 saw yet further innovation when the *Kennel Gazette* for that month also became the official Crufts Souvenir Guide providing all the information visitors to Crufts could possibly require, be they pet owners, or experienced dog breeders and exhibitors.

The ever growing popularity of canine events and the increasingly high profile of the pet industry in general has seen the expansion of the *Gazette's* editorial brief still further. September, 1998, heralded the *Gazette's* latest reincarnation with a new, integrated and modern design for a progressive and professional magazine. Today's *Gazette* provides its readers with intelligent and in-depth articles about canine genetics, hereditary diseases, the latest news from the pet industry, detailed reports of shows, field trials, working trials, agility and flyball competitions, a section devoted to the Kennel Club Junior Organisation, an informed letters page, celebrity interviews, veterinary articles, dog training issues, dogs and the law, book reviews, canine collectables and, as all the best adverts say, all this and much, much more!

So the story of the Kennel Club *Stud Book* shows how it was one of the most important reasons for the formation of the Kennel Club itself. It is still as important today, for within its pages are the framework of British dogdom from 1859 to 2000.

Valerie Foss.

Standards to which dogs are judged

*D*OGS *are judged* against the standard for their particular breeds. Judges will equate in their minds how well a dog compares with its standard and the dog which, in the judge's opinion, is best matched to the standard will win its class, group or, perhaps, even best in show.

There are many points to be considered and each breed standard sets out the requirements for various parts of the anatomy; for example, the Boston Terrier:

Ears carried erect; small, thin, situated as near corner of skull as possible.

or for the German Shepherd:

Mouth, Jaws strongly developed. With a perfect, regular and complete, scissor bite, ie upper teeth closely overlapping lower teeth and set square to the jaws. Teeth healthy and strong. Full dentition desirable.

The Kennel Club recognises 192 different breeds of dog and each breed has its own descriptive standard. It is a word picture or specification which details the animal's essential features. Usually a standard is based on that recognised in a breed's native country, a system agreed by a conference of world kennel clubs.

The Breed Standards and Stud Book sub-committee of the Kennel Club consists of ten members, elected according to the Rules of the Kennel Club and includes one veterinary surgeon who is a member of the Kennel Club but elected by the Kennel Club/British Small Animals Veterinary Association Scientific Committee.

The function of the sub-committee is to consider and advise on any matters concerned with the recognition of breeds, breed standards, genetic aspects of dogs and artificial insemination as well as the content of the *Stud Book*.

The breed standards are published in loose leaf form but there is also a coffee table version of the *Illustrated Breed Standards,* published by the Kennel Club, which is considered the official guide to all registered breeds and was last updated in 1998. In this each breed carries a colour photograph to support the text. On the following page is a sample standard (English Setter).

Bernard Hall.

Arthur Wardle (1864-1949). 'The Pick of the Kennel'. This painting was purchased in 1996 to increase the breeds represented in the collection. Signed and inscribed, oil on canvas, 16" x 22".

83

The dog should fit the standard – English Setter

General Appearance Of medium height, clean in outline, elegant in appearance and movement.

Characteristics Very active with a keen game sense.

Temperament Intensely friendly and good natured.

Head and Skull Head carried high, long and reasonably lean, with well defined stop. Skull oval from ear to ear, showing plenty of brain room, a well defined occipital protuberance. Muzzle moderately deep and fairly square, from stop to point of nose, should equal length of skull from occiput to eyes, nostrils wide and jaws of nearly equal length, flews not too pendulous, colour of nose black or liver, according to colour of coat.

Illustrated is the male record holder in English Setters Sh.Ch. Elswood Vagabond King (40 CCs)

Eyes Bright, mild and expressive. Colour ranging between hazel and dark brown, the darker the better. In liver beltons only, a lighter eye acceptable. Eyes oval and not protruding.

Ears Moderate length, set on low, and hanging in neat folds close to cheek, tip velvety, upper part clothed in fine silky hair.

Mouth Jaws strong, with a perfect, regular and complete scissor bite, i.e. upper teeth closely overlapping lower teeth and set square to the jaws. Full dentition desirable.

Neck Rather long, muscular and lean, slightly arched at crest, and clean-cut where it joins head, towards shoulders larger and very muscular, never throaty nor pendulous below throat, but elegant in appearance.

Forequarters Shoulders well set back or oblique, chest deep in brisket, very good depth and width between shoulder blades, forearms straight and very muscular with rounded bone, elbows well let down close to body, pasterns short, strong, round and straight.

Body Moderate length, back short and level with good round widely sprung ribs and deep in back ribs, i.e. well ribbed up.

Hindquarters Loins wide, slightly arched, strong and muscular, legs well muscled including second thigh, stifles well bent and thighs long from hip to hock, hock inclining neither in nor out and well let down.

Feet Well padded, tight, with close well arched toes protected by hair between them.

Tail Set almost in line with back, medium length, not reaching below hock, neither curly nor ropy, slightly curved or scimitar-shaped but with no tendency to turn upwards: flag or feathers hanging in long pendant flakes. Feather commencing slightly below the root, and increasing in length towards middle, then gradually tapering towards end, hair long, bright, soft and silky, wavy but not curly. Lively and slashing in movement and carried in a plane not higher than level of back.

Gait/Movement Free and graceful action, suggesting speed and endurance. Free movement of the hock showing powerful drive from hindquarters. Viewed from rear, hip, stifle and hock joints in line. Head naturally high.

Coat From back of head in line with ears slightly wavy, not curly, long and silky as is coat generally, breeches and forelegs nearly down to feet well feathered.

Colour Black and white (blue belton), orange and white (orange belton), lemon and white (lemon belton), liver and white (liver belton) or tricolour, that is blue belton and tan or liver belton and tan, those without heavy patches of colour on body but flecked (belton) all over preferred.

Size Height: dogs: 65-68 cms (25 $^1/_2$-27 ins); bitches: 61-65 cms (24-25 $^1/_2$ ins).

Faults Any departure from the foregoing points should be considered a fault and the seriousness with which the fault should be regarded should be in exact proportion to its degree.

Note Male animals should have two apparently normal testicles fully descended into the scrotum.

Kennel Club involved in genetics since 1945

THE deliberate breeding of any species of mammal is governed by genetic influence. This fact has to be recognised by all who set out to breed "pure-bred" animals and certainly applies to all those who breed pedigree dogs.

Dog breeding, in the days before a handful of qualified geneticists became interested in the dog as a species, was entirely in the hands of men and women who decided on the matings within their own breeding-strains; they studied pedigrees and looked at the dogs and bitches available in either the working field or the show-ring. Their degree of success in this was governed by their ability to note what traits were passed on regularly from one generation to the next and use that information to their own and their dogs' benefit.

The first apparent involvement of "genetics" in the world of dogs in the United Kingdom dates from the pioneering work of W.J. (Bill) Rasbridge, secretary of the Irish Setter Association of England (ISAE), who identified the condition of Night Blindness or Progressive Retinal Atrophy (PRA).

He persuaded not only his fellow breeders, but also the members of the General Committee of the Kennel Club as long ago as 1945, that the registrations of both actively affected dogs and carriers of the recessive gene should be cancelled. Test-mating was the path by which the breed was virtually cleared of the condition in those early days – a drastic method, but extremely effective as it turned out.

Times have changed to the extent that there are now many eye-defects which can be diagnosed by those highly skilled in the use of opthalmoscopes. The Kennel Club, the British Veterinary Association and the International Sheep Dog Society combine to run an official scheme under which some 50 recognised referees examine the eyes of dogs and bitches and publish the results of their examinations, good or bad, quarterly through the *Breed Supplements to the Stud Book*.

In parallel with these eye-schemes, the Kennel Club and the British Veterinary Association have initiated schemes to assist breeders in controlling such orthopaedic problems as hip-dysplasia and elbow-dysplasia. Once again the results are published in order that all breeders will be able to assess the degree of defect in those dogs or bitches which they consider using in their own breeding programmes.

The sciences of canine genetics and micro-biology made rapid advances in the second half of the 20th Century and particularly in its fourth quarter. The micro-structure of those cells of which animal bodies are composed has been "broken down" to the extent that we now talk in terms of the DNA (deoxyribonucleic acid) structure of the genes carried on chromosomes which transmits the necessary genetic information by which a dog replicates itself in the next generation. Modern dog-breeders are in an age in which they can, in some cases, recognise the carrier-state which has hitherto plagued their efforts to "breed away" from inherited defects without adopting the "unacceptable" idea of test-mating.

Bill Rasbridge

In all this progress The Kennel Club has been playing a more and more active part by encouraging much research at veterinary and medical institutes, both financially through its own Kennel Club Charitable Trust and by publishing information originating from those institutes, be they university veterinary teaching faculties or such research-orientated concerns as the Animal Health Trust.

This is a far cry from the original concept of those who founded the Kennel Club in 1873, but is still a true advance of one of the major aims of those Founding Fathers, the improvement of dogs.

Dr. Jeff Sampson BSc DPhil, Kennel Club Canine Genetics Co-ordinator, appointed April 1998.

One of the most intriguing "Treasures of The Kennel Club" is that its membership today includes men and women interested in the many varied facets of the study and keeping of dogs. There are among the ranks of the breeders/fanciers of the recognised breeds of pure-bred dogs a number of veterinary surgeons and geneticists. Their specialised viewpoint has been utilised by the club not only within the General Committee, but in the Breed Standards and Stud Book Sub-Committee and more particularly in the Kennel Club/British Small Animal Veterinary Association (KC/BSAVA) Joint Scientific Committee.

Increasingly breeders and breed clubs are turning for help and advice to the Kennel Club in a fashion which would have been almost unknown in the first 70 or more years of its existence.

Problems caused by genetic abnormalities or defects were undoubtedly suspected in those earlier years, but in the face of the evidence exposed often by junior breeders, the senior breeders exhibited some degree of reluctance to take note and many a carpet was pulled back at the corner in order that disturbing news could be conveniently swept underneath!

It would be facile to suggest that such concealment no longer occurs, but undoubtedly the tide of research into canine micro-biology coupled with the open publication of accurate results in such publications as the *Kennel Gazette,* the *Veterinary Record* and the *Journal of Small Animal Practice* today leaves few hiding-places for those who try to conceal breed defects from the public gaze.

The laws of the land also now cover dishonest attempts to sell dogs suffering from the defect(s) known to occur in the particular breed unless the vendor has made a serious attempt to "breed away" from the defect(s).

In addition to all these advances, the Kennel Club has taken the lead in calling together representatives from veterinary schools and other centres of excellence, as well as from the dedicated canine press, those commercial firms

London Laughs: Kennel Club
'No Sir! It doesn't make you a member just because you have an air-raid shelter in your back garden.' (Lee)

with a particular affinity to the dog, and from the British Veterinary Association and the Royal College of Veterinary Surgeons, in order to discuss the possibility of creating some point of co-ordination of knowledge of the inherited disease in the dog.

The end result of these discussions, as they progressed, was the setting-up and funding of the post of Kennel Club Genetics Co-ordinator, a position held by Dr. Jeff Sampson. This has to be seen as a great step forward in the Kennel Club's pursuit of its primary objective – the betterment of the health of the dog.

Mike Stockman.

Championships
and the rules

THE first Kennel Club show is well recorded in canine literature, not only how it came about, but also concerning the early committee members and the running of the show. It was at the Crystal Palace, London, over a four-day period from June 17-20, 1873, with entries numbering 975 dogs.

Published in the first *Stud Book* of 1859-1874 was the first set of a *"code of rules for the guidance of dog shows"*. The ten rules included for instance *"if a dog was entered without being clearly identified he forfeited any prize awarded."* The same disqualification also for *"any dog exhibited with a different name to which it was last exhibited, unless notice had been given to the secretary at the time of entry"*. The dog had to be shown under both old and new names until the publication of the *Kennel Calendar,* where the change of name was recorded. Another rule of interest was *"In estimating the number of prizes a dog has won with reference to whether it should compete in a Champion class or not, the number of prizes won should be calculated up to the morning of the show, and not merely to the date of entry."*

Prior to 1877 champion classes were provided at shows for various breeds, but there appear to be no definite regulations, - nor as far as can be traced, did the Kennel Club seem to have formulated any rules concerning them. The first mention of champion classes appears to be at the **"First Great International Dog Show"** in 1863, held at the Agricultural Hall, Islington, where 1678 dogs were entered, but as the entries in many cases comprised several dogs, (one owner irrespective of the number of dogs counted as one entry) in all probability there were over 2,000 dogs actually at the show. The five champion classes scheduled were for the following breeds:

Champion class Bloodhounds
won by Mr Jennings' *DRUID*

Champion class Greyhounds
won by Mr Spinks' *SEAFOAM*

Champion class Pointers (Large size)
won by Mr Newton's *RANGER*

Champion class Pointers (Small size)
won by Mr Bayley's *DASH*

Champion class English Setters
won by Mr Ellery's *ARGYLL II*

The subject of champions was first debated by the Kennel Club in July 1877, when it was decided that the title of champion could not be assumed until a dog had won three prizes. In 1880 this championship rule appeared in the official Kennel Club rules and now stated *"No dog or bitch shall be entitled to be called a Champion that has not won 4 first prizes at shows registered in the stud book. One of the 4 first prizes being in a Champion class, (an extra prize for the best of two or more classes.) A prize in a variety class or a prize in a class for puppies under 12 months old shall not count as a win."*

The four wins before being entitled to be called a champion, remained until 1885, when the number was increased to seven. Diverging a little, it is of interest that the first stewards were appointed to assist judges in the ring in 1879. These seven named gentlemen thus go down in history as the first in a long line of these most necessary of helpers to a judge. Also in 1880 a new definition came into being, regarding unlicensed show wins not being able to be counted towards a championship, and was the subject of quite some protest by the dog press! Members of the Kennel Club were asked to abstain from judging or exhibiting at shows not held under Kennel Club rules. A long time prior to 1882 the Kennel Club published particulars of various shows not held under their rules in the stud books and from that year they ceased to recognise shows not held under their rules and regulations.

The vexing question of championships continued to be debated up to 1884. The few shows held under Kennel Club rules each year made it comparatively easy to safeguard the importance of the title of champion, but with the increase of shows the opportunities for winning championship honours also had proportionally increased. Many prominent dog owners objected to the conditions under which the honour could be gained. They asserted that it was far too easy

First Prize card from Crufts 1891, held at the Agricultural Hall, London.

and simple to gain a coveted title. This objection was based on the rule that a dog winning three 1st prizes under the rules was eligible to compete in a champion class, and after winning that class once, became a champion and remained so for life. A further point was that with astute management the honour could be secured with the minimum of opposition.

A First Prize card awarded to Mr. F. D. George's Irish Wolfhound "Garryowen" at the Kennel Club's 35th Show, April 1891.

In those days many of the shows adopted the sweepstakes principle, with no added money from the society or club to be given to the winner, all the prize money coming from the exhibitors' entry money, so that an obscure show (for at that time the consent of the Kennel Club to provide challenge classes was not necessary) could put on a challenge class without any extra expense. It was possible that with only one entry in such a class, a dog might win the money staked by its owner; not meet any opposition yet obtain the coveted title of champion. Owners and the dog press suggested various remedies. One journal argued that "old age, complete loss of form and shape, even the absence of a limb in a Pointer or Setter, or the nose from a Retriever or Spaniel, an ear or the teeth missing from a Fox Terrier, the tail from a Pug, or the deprivation of sight

from a Greyhound, would not remove them from the role of Champion, which prior to their misfortune had been acquired."

The debate went on at some length: "No more foolish would it seem to have our Champion mile runner with a wooden leg than it does to have our Champion Setter with his nose cut off, or a Greyhound stone blind. An athlete loses his title on suffering defeat and becomes an "Ex" Champion. when once a dog attains the dignity he carries it to the end of his days, however much he may, with increasing years, become transformed from a once noble creature into a miserable specimen of decrepitude."

The editor of the *Kennel Gazette* replied to some of the criticisms that had been made. "It is very apparent that if the means are too easy for attaining Champion honours when about 20 shows come under acknowledged rules, the facilities become quite alarming when the list numbers 50 or 60, the prestige belonging to the term Champion should be strictly maintained, every right thinking owner of dogs will agree with us in that opinion."

The General Committee also decided that a prize in a selling class (dogs were often sold for their catalogue price from a "selling" class) should not count as a win when calculating the points for the title of champion. Before a dog could compete in a challenge class, it must have won not less than four first prizes at Kennel Club shows. Where challenge classes were provided, no dog eligible for that class could be shown in an open class. In order to gain the title of champion the dog must have won seven prizes at Rule shows, (i.e. shows held under KC Rules), three such prizes being in the challenge classes, and one at least being at the Birmingham or Kennel Club shows.

The following year it was made mandatory that the four other wins must come from open classes. In 1889 a further clause was added, that all dogs entered for competition and actually in the show **"may not be withdrawn from competition without the sanction of the committee or secretary"**. The circumstances of this rule being put into place came about by the judge of Newfoundlands at Birmingham 1889, complaining that on going round the benches after judging, he found **Black Prince** in his proper place (i.e. benched) although he had not been brought into the ring to be judged. He had been informed the dog was not present, and had therefore given the Challenge prize to *Alderman,* Black Prince's kennel companion. The inference being that Black Prince had been wilfully withdrawn from competition.

The St.Bernard Club tardily applied to hold their shows under Kennel Club rules that year. St. Bernards drew huge entries at that time with dogs bought and sold for enormous prices. For example at the club's winter show held over three days in December 1887, 226 dogs competed in 24 classes, prices ranged from £6.6s for *Albula,* £104 for *Refuge II* plus four services free, and £10,000 for *Angelo* (imported).

Further changes in the qualifying points towards the championship title were not made until 1889. The Kennel Club then selected a list of shows worthy of being ranked as "First class" exhibitions, and a first prize won at one of these shows for the purpose of challenge class qualifications, counted as two points. A first won at any other show held under rules was worth one point. No dog could compete in a challenge class until he had won ten points at these listed shows. They had all to be awarded from open classes, which were open to all dogs without restrictions. Where challenge classes were provided no dog qualified for this class could be exhibited in the open class. (A similar situation exists today in most all shows abroad.) These were the rules applying to be eligible for a challenge class.

To become a champion, a dog had to win six points in challenge classes, two of which had to be at either the Kennel Club's own shows or at the National Dog Show Society, Birmingham. The same points, i.e. "two" and "one" were to apply to the shows, depending upon the show's grading. If a dog was disqualified from a win, the next dog in place order took the prize. Equal first prizes often confuses people researching early champions, but an equal prize counted as a win for both dogs. These rules came into effect on January 1, 1889, but any dog having qualified for a champion or challenge class before that date would have to compete in a challenge class thereafter.

Around the same time a certain Mr. Treweeks' appeal was heard. Mr Treweeks sent his Collie *Cyclops,* to the Ebbw Vale show, where the judge awarded him a first and the cup for the best Collie in the show, and claimed him at his

catalogue price of £20. Mr Treweeks telegraphed to the secretary asking what success his dog had, and received a reply to the effect that he gained a first and the cup, and had been sold to the judge at the catalogue price. On the day after the show his Collie was returned to him, and he immediately telegraphed for an explanation, receiving the reply that the judge had thought the Collie was a bitch and had judged it accordingly. On discovering his error, however, he re-judged the class, gave the cup to another and cancelled his purchase. Evidence was given as to the manner in which the error arose, and the committee unanimously decided that a judge had the right to re-judge a class!

The front of the solid silver medal given by the Kennel Club to the winner of Challenge Classes at their own show.

In 1889 the new rules had been in effect for just six weeks before the annual general meeting of the Kennel Club. On the whole they were favourably received, but nearly everyone at the meeting agreed there should be a further restriction on dogs progressing towards an easy title of champion. The "First" and "Second" class show classification were classified solely according to whether the entries at shows reached a certain minimum number, but this was felt to be greatly misunderstood by both the dog exhibitors and the general public, who thought that a "First" class show had better quality dogs than a "Second". Kennel Club members at this annual meeting decided to amend Rule 15 to change the words "First Class Exhibitions" to "Two point shows" and Second Class to One Point. This removed the offensive First and Second and substituted Two point and One point shows.

Inscription reads: The Kennel Club's 36th Show 1892, 1st Prize Challenge Class awarded to Mr. F. D. George's Irish Wolfhound "Garryowen" (The third champion in the breed).

Mr. F. D. George and his Irish Wolfhound Ch.Garryowen 1892.

So in 1890, the first of the new two point shows were held - the shows selected for this status were: The Kennel Club shows, Birmingham, Brighton, Darlington, Dublin, Edinburgh, Gloucester, Liverpool, Manchester,

The Pug Dog, St.Bernard, Collie, Poodle, Fox Terrier and Toy Spaniel clubs. In 1891 the Scottish Kennel Club successfully lobbied to be added to the list, and put on the same level as Birmingham for purposes of championship shows. The same year the Bulldog Club also was added to the list of two point shows. At this time the business of the Kennel Club had increased to such an extent that it was proposed to hold fortnightly meetings instead of the monthly meetings. Appeals and disqualifications were numerous as more and more specialist clubs decided to come under the wing of the Kennel Club.

First Prize card from the Kennel Club's 37th Show at the Crystal Palace, October 1893.

In 1891 even more specialist clubs were selected to rank along side the Kennel Club, Birmingham and Edinburgh shows as Two point shows. These shows were gradually extended to include others, but in that year the favoured clubs were the Fox Terrier Club, the St.Bernard Club, the Collie Club, and the Bulldog Club.

Second Prize card awarded to HRH Edward Prince of Wales' Basset Hound at the Kennel Club's 38th Show, Crystal Palace April 1894.

One lovely story concerning a disqualification of an Irish Water Spaniel owned by Mr. Carnac Tisdall, namely **Free O'Donoghue,** was reported in the *Kennel Gazette* during 1892. The judge, well after judging had finished, withheld the prize in the challenge class, to which Free O'Donoghue was entitled, being the only entry. The judge stated he had carefully examined the dog in the ring, and after noting various points, signified his intention of awarding him the prize. Later, when passing the benches, he was struck with what appeared to him to be a blemish on the dog's nose. It being dark at the time he struck a match, and on close examination came to the conclusion that the nose must have been blemished at the time of judging. He called the veterinary surgeon who reported that the dog's nose was blemished, in his opinion the result of an injury of some standing, and that the judge must have failed to notice it when the dog was in the ring. The committee allowed Mr Tisdall's appeal as they said it was obvious the dog had been shown with a parti-coloured nose, and this had escaped the notice of the judge, Col. Trench.

Show rules were not amended again until 1893, giving show committees the power to schedule any classes they liked, but limiting records in the *Calendar and Stud Book* to winners of prizes in "Winners" and "Open" classes. "Winners" was limited to dogs of any breed or variety which had previously won one or more first prizes in an open class, and open classes for dogs in which no previous prize winner was debarred from competing, except when winners classes were provided for that breed.

Rule 16 allowed winners and open classes to be limited by weight, colour, height, sex or age. Rule 17 did away with Two point shows and substituted championship shows. Only eight shows were so ranked at the beginning, the Kennel Club show, Birkenhead, the South London Bulldog Soc., the Fox Terrier Club, Birmingham, Liverpool, Derby and Dublin.

Nothing in 1894 was eventful for fresh legislation, the principal alteration was drawing up regulations as to which classes would count for entry into the *Stud Book*. "Winners" and "Open" already qualified but it was decided to add "Limit" to these. Limit classes were for all dogs which had not won four first prizes. In the same year the well-known bulldog fancier, Mr Edgar Farman, suggested that the Kennel Club should issue official certificates of championship for dogs entitled to that distinction but the committee came to no decision on the subject.

In 1897 an important decision was given by the committee in a case where the judge at the Leicester show had awarded equal firsts to the Great Danes in the open bitch class- **Champion Mammoth** and **Lore of Redgrave** and subsequently gave them an equal championship. The secretary of the show asked for directions as to how this question was to be dealt with. The judge's explanation was that having placed these two bitches equal first in a previous class he could not do otherwise than again place them equal for the championship prize. The committee decided that the championship prize could only be given to the best dog of the breed in the show, and as the judge had failed to separate the two dogs no championship prize could be awarded.

No more tinkering of the rules was contemplated until 1900. Mr Edgar Farman proposed the substitution of the name "Kennel Club Challenge prizes or certificates", instead of the misleading "Champion prize or Certificate." The latter term had led to misconception on the part of the public, as many thought that a dog became a champion by winning a single "Champion prize" not understanding the distinction between a championship win and the title of champion. The need for accentuating the distinction was at once seen and Mr Farman's proposition was carried unanimously.

On Jan 1, 1904, a rule came into force that three challenge prizes or certificates had to be won under at least three different judges, the judge however was at liberty to withhold the award if there was not a dog of sufficient merit present. After the beginning of 1903 no shows which gave prizes on the sweepstakes principle or which offered prize money in all classes of less than £2 for a first prize were eligible for challenge prizes.

Single CCs

Right through these formative years the challenge certificates or prizes had been awarded either singly for best of breed or one for each sex. This sensible idea could well be revived today to the benefit of some of our minority breeds. The sexes could compete together, if the classification was small, but an open class had to be provided in all cases where challenges were on offer. Championship shows in 1905 numbered 32, this included the few specialist clubs which were allowed their own championship shows. By 1906 the wording "Challenge Certificate" was then in general use and the "Challenge Prize" dropped out of use. In 1907 the rules stated that a maximum number of CCs per breed in any one year would not exceed 20, apart from the four representative shows.

The sub-committee set up to investigate and amend the rules for gundogs qualifying in both field and bench put forward the recommendation that Pointers, Setters, Sporting Spaniels and Retrievers, born after June 1, 1909, in addition to winning three CCs must also have gained a prize or certificate of merit at a field trial recognised by the Kennel Club, before being qualified for the title of champion. Equal awards were still recognised, but it was becoming increasingly unusual to find two dogs of any breed placed equal in the *Stud Book*.

At the onset of the First World War, things went on much as before, though in 1914 the compulsory payment of a minimum of £2 for first prize, and other prize money was suspended, as in many cases championship shows were connected to war charities. For the first time a regulation was proposed to provide a "reserve" for a challenge certificate, where the judge thought there was sufficient merit. In deciding such awards, the judge had to consider the question of bringing into the ring second prize winners, to compete for this new award. This rule came into effect in 1915, and was named the Reserve Best of Sex Award.

Reserve Prize card from the 39th Kennel Club Show at the Crystal Palace in October 1894.

Even after the war had been raging for 17 months, the dog showing fraternity had managed to stage 475 shows, although the Kennel Club's own show, due to be held at Olympia in December, had to be abandoned. During 1917 the number of shows had dropped to 135, of which just six were championship shows. Registrations had dropped to a handful under special licence from the Kennel Club, and the Government viewed with great disfavour any relaxation over the reduced number of breeding licences granted. At the end of the year the Government banned the holding of shows altogether, but after representations from the Kennel Club they allowed the holding of "restricted" or "radius" shows.

The six championship shows held in 1917 were at Edinburgh (Caledonian Canine Soc.), Accrington (North-East Lancashire Pomeranian Club), Manchester (Northern Collie Club), London (Wire Fox Terrier Ass), London (Cruft's Great Dog Show), Manchester (The Collie Club).

The most disastrous year that had ever afflicted dogdom was 1918. Resulting from pressure from the Government, restrictions on breeding were even more stringently enforced. Radius shows were limited to dogs which had been kept for a minimum of three months, within a radius of ten miles of the venue. No championship shows were held, and the whole population struggled to keep their dogs and their spirits up, until the Armistice was declared in November. Dog breeding was allowed by the government to be resumed after November 22 and some show licences were granted by the Kennel Club for the following year. Unfortunately an outbreak of rabies prevented some of these early 1919 shows being held; restrictions on the movement of dogs and a partial muzzling order imposed. The situation gradually improved with over 100 open shows and well over that number of sanction shows being held.

The Kennel Club Challenge Certificate won at Crufts 1925 by the King Charles Spaniel Little Minaster.

Just two championship events were staged during the year, both in London and both the Great Joint Terrier Shows.

As the single challenge certificate for best of breed only had fallen out of favour and the plan was quickly to build up the devastated dog owning community, challenge certificates were on offer for both sexes, and in every breed. This rule was to come into force in 1920. Judges were still not restricted too much and the only rule pertaining to them at championship shows was that they were allowed to award challenge certificates in the same breed only four times in any one year. They also had to be an authority on the breed, or their qualifications for judging the breed had to be submitted to the Kennel Club. Permission to hold a championship show was not granted to any specialist club unless the registrations in the previous year totalled more than 125 dogs.

Forty-one championship shows in 1921 set the dog scene well on its way again. In 1925 an important recommendation was submitted to Kennel Club members for their decision, in reference to the classification of prizes. Mr William McCandlish said "the original idea of "Grand Challenge prizes" was for a prize to be open to all exhibitors. Some people had been using the word so they might charge an entrance fee and make it a grand challenge class. The result was that people had been winning prizes, intimating that they had been winning at such and such shows, and the public had imagined that particular dog was best in the show, whereas it was often best of a poor class at the show".

It was decided that a paragraph should be added after the existing regulation to read as follows :- *"The words Grand, Champion, or Challenge must not be used in the designation of any class or prize for which an entrance fee is charged, and for which entry has to be made prior to the day of the show."* In order that sufficient notice might be given to all show committees, the revision of the rule was not to be enforced until January 1, 1926.

Also at the same meeting it was resolved that the rule be made to read as follows: *"a dog should not obtain a Challenge Certificate unless it has won a prize in a class confined to its recognised breed or variety, and open to all exhibitors at the show in question".* This alteration brings back the wording of the rule as it read prior to October 19, 1924. The next regulation of interest was: *"No breed shall be entitled to apply for Championship status for a specialist show unless there shall have been at least 1000 registrations in that breed during the preceding calendar year."*

It was also ruled that any breed on the register of recognised breeds which had forfeited challenge certificates by falling below 20 registrations in the preceding year, should become entitled to challenge certificates the following year if in any year it attained 20 registrations.

The question of providing standard award cards for best and reserve best in each sex was considered, and the following resolution was passed in 1930: *"That at all open shows at which Challenge Certificates are given, the judges of each breed mark award slips of best of each sex and reserve to same, and that distinctive award cards for "best" and "reserve best" of an approved general form and design be issued by Show Executives."*

It was further decided to issue (to come into operation on January 1, 1931) the following instructions to show secretaries: *"for Best of sex in Breed at championship shows, red, white and red; for Reserve best of sex in Breed at championship shows, green, white and green. The colours red, blue, yellow and green must not be used for any other award cards".* It was not until this particular year, that judges were requested to place the first four winning dogs in order in the ring, when making their awards.

A comparison of registrations to the number of Champions is interesting and is as follows:

1925 Registrations 55,529		1939 Registrations 36,124	
Breeds on Reg.	74	Breeds on Reg.	90
Ch. Shows	47	Ch.Shows	39
New Chs.	230	New Chs.	253

The average number of new champions per breed per year between these years was 3.5.

In 1932 Colonel Claude Cane died. Well-known in all dog related matters, he was a prolific writer and sportsman. He was responsible for the legislation, which came into force in January 1899 that "all the shows not held under KC rules should be regarded as unrecognised shows, and dogs competing at such shows are to be disqualified from competing at shows held under Kennel Club rules". At the time this far reaching and important regulation was made, there were actually more unrecognised shows than shows held under the aegis of the Kennel Club. This new rule speedily put an end to the existence of the unrecognised shows. During 1933 the General Committee of the Kennel Club accepted the recommendation that the challenge certificate award card should have printed on it *"I am clearly of the opinion that No _____ is of such outstanding merit as to be worthy of the title of Champion."*

A separate register for Australian Terriers was granted in this year and they had also qualified for the minimum number of challenge certificates of four per year. At this time, the judging of breeds in which challenge certificates were offered had to commence not later than 11.30am, and had to have priority over all other breeds and classes. No variety classes were able to be judged before the challenge certificate breeds had been completed. At last the committee also changed the regulation that the interval of three months between awards of challenge certificates by the same judge, should be increased to six months. This was thought to be a well overdue and welcome piece of legislation.

It is sad to record the burning in 1936 of the Crystal Palace during the evening of November 30, when this unique building, the scene of so many successful Kennel Club shows, was reduced in two hours, to a twisted mass of ironwork and broken glass. The fire was the greatest that London had witnessed for many years, and genuine regret was felt at the passing of a familiar and famous landmark, the home of so many exhibitions and shows of all descriptions. The Palace was always the favourite venue of the Kennel Club show, 53 of which took place under its glass roof.

Breeders' diplomas were first issued for the breeder of all dogs which obtained their title, from September 7, 1937 and this proved to be most popular. Early in 1937 a number of French Bulldog owners joined together to subscribe for the purchase of a perpetual trophy to be kept by the Kennel Club. It was to be awarded to the French Bulldog taking the largest number of challenge certificates during each year. The trophy was given in memory of the late Mrs Gwendoline Romilly whose interest in, and knowledge of French Bulldogs, was so well known and widely appreciated.

The style of the Challenge Certificate has been unchanged for decades. Here is one from 1933, won by the St. Bernard, Beldene Bruno.

In 1938 a regulation was introduced that a dog should not be able to obtain a CC (challenge certificate) unless it had won a prize in mid-limit, limit or open class at a show. It was announced that the regulation would come into force on Jan 1, 1939, but after a "U" turn by the Kennel Club, it was rescinded in November 1938, to the great relief of the exhibitors.

The Junior Warrant was also introduced this year, hopefully to provide some reliable indication of the quality of young stock. The first award sent out from the Kennel Club was to Mr H. Lloyd's Cocker Spaniel bitch Fair Choice of Ware. She secured the necessary points at just two championship shows, Crufts and Glasgow. During the year no less than 60 of these valuable and prestigious junior warrants were issued.

At the outbreak of the Second World War in 1939 it was feared that the activities of the

Kennel Club would be greatly curtailed. A large number of shows were immediately cancelled, including the club's own show, which was to have been held on December 6 and 7. Field trials, too, were abandoned, and the number of registrations declined rapidly. The then secretary reported that ten crates containing all the General Committee minute books from 1874 onwards, a number of interesting dog show catalogues of the sixties and seventies, and sets of the *Stud Book* and *Kennel Gazette* had been sent down to Kent, for safe custody during the war.

There were 55 championship shows held during 1939 together with more than 100 open

An early Champion Certificate of 1934

shows, around 50 limited shows and hundreds of sanction shows and matches. However, at the end of the year championship shows were suspended indefinitely and 1940 saw further great curtailment of canine affairs. Committee meetings were held for emergency reasons only and in February an appeal was made to all dog owners to breed as few litters as possible during the duration of the war.

Alterations to the rules regarding the exhibition of challenge certificate winners at shows other than championship were made; they were allowed to compete at limited and sanction shows held by specialist clubs. This alteration was a temporary measure designed to meet the prevailing conditions. As usual the dog fancy all pulled together and formed a " Dog Fighters Fund". A cheque for the whole amount raised was sent to Lord Beaverbrook with the request that the aeroplane the money bought might be named *"The Dog Fighter".* Two photographs of the aeroplane purchased by all the dog breeders were published in the September issue of the *Kennel Gazette.* Happily, 1945 saw the end of the disastrous war in which the whole country had been engaged for the last six years, but the many hampering restrictions and difficulties which it inevitably brought in its wake had by no means disappeared. Although enemy action was no longer to be feared, conditions during the six months after

hostilities ceased were no easier than they had been during the time when fighting was in progress. Still the number of shows in 1945 kept up and over 1200 open, limited and sanction shows were held.

The Kennel Club hoped that championship shows could be resumed as soon as possible, but only when adequate benching, sufficient food and water utensils became available. These necessities could be provided only when permission was given by the relevant authorities for labour and materials. Until that was done, the chairman stated, the Kennel Club would be powerless. Radius restrictions of 25 miles for shows were still in place, and the Kennel Club could not get the government to agree to a relaxation of this rule until the end of July that year.

Championship shows recommenced with the Dachshund Club on May 1, 1946. The revival of Crufts was possible in 1947, it produced a good entry of 4,273 dogs, and an attendance of 50,000 by the public helped make this a record for dog shows anywhere throughout the world. Also in 1947, to achieve an entry in the *Stud Book* the rules were amended to include challenge certificate winners, reserve best of sex, first, second and third prize winners in open or limit classes at championship shows where CC's were on offer.

The old Reserve Best of Sex card replaced in 1978

Show entries continued to increase over the subsequent years and various small "tweakings" of the rules were put in place, but essentially the show world was set for honest and fair competition to take it through the post war years and up to the present day. In 1978 the first actual reserve challenge certificates were issued, although exhibitors had long called the runner up to the CC winner by this name. Previously the reserve CC winner, or reserve "ticket" winner, had been officially referred to as the Reserve Best of Sex award. Exhibitors really

THE KENNEL CLUB

THE KENNEL CLUB
1 Clarges Street, London W1Y 8AB

KENNEL CLUB AWARD CARD FOR

BEST OF BREED

Breed _____ Sex _____
Name of Exhibit _____
Signed _____
Judge

appreciated the new name and design of the award card which was more worthy of being framed than its predecessor.

A new style junior warrant has now been introduced to both help the open shows and make the award even more highly sought after. Now a minimum of 12 of the 25 points have to be won at championship shows where CCs are on offer, and the same number of points at either championship shows without CCs, or open shows. There must be a minimum number of three dogs present in the class to claim the points; three points at CC shows, and one point for the other shows. The title of "junior warrant" may be used after the name of the dog in show catalogues, and a competition

to find the top junior warrant winner of the year with regional heats is held near the end of each year. A junior warrant holder will be awarded a number in the *Stud Book*.

In 1999 the General Committee approved "new look" award cards, in both design and shape. These came into use as from January 1, 2000.

This brings us up to date at the time of publication but who can say when the complicated and constantly changing rules and regulations will alter yet again? Not me.

Zena Thorn-Andrews

The Kennel Club has in its possession a number of cartoons poking gentle fun at the club. Some can be found scattered through this book.

'Do you know you're sitting on my Chihuahua?' (Giles)

'You of course, had to be different. You had to go and pick the judge up by his ears'. (Giles)

When registration cost just 5p

*E*VEN *the most basic* civilisation has language and language starts with names for things rather than the discussion of ideas. As soon as there was more than one dog associated with the tribe it was necessary for there to be a name for each. One would be faster than the other and was probably known as "Speedy". One would be stronger than the other and probably be the ubiquitous "Butch". With a bit of luck, or maybe intentionally, they would mate and one of the progeny would be the first of the canine double barrelled names "Speedy Butch".

The Kennel Club started to record the names of dogs that had earned an award in competition as soon as it was formed in 1873 and another chapter records the start of the *Stud Book*. It was not until 1880 that it became necessary to register every dog that was to be entered in Kennel Club licensed competition. Human nature being what it is this was necessary to control some of the shenanigans that had been taking place at shows.

The regulations for registration were only four. (Would that things were so simple today)

1. Every dog exhibited at a show held under Kennel Club Rules must, previous to the time of entry for such show, be entered in a registry of names kept by the Kennel Club at their office, 29a, Pall Mall, London, S.W.

2. A charge of one shilling each dog will be made for registration (one shilling equates to 5p today).

3. A name that has already been assumed and duly registered in the Kennel Club Registry, or entered in any published number of *The Kennel Club Calendar and Stud Book,* by the owner of a dog of the same breed, cannot be registered unless by a distinguishing name or number.

4. Dogs that are already entered in any published number of *The Kennel Club Calendar and Stud Book* are exempt from the above rule, provided their names remain unchanged.

Throughout the history of the registration system the names of dogs have reflected various aspects of the society that owned them or the nature of the dog's function in that society. Of the first four Bloodhounds registered and published in the first *Gazette* in April 1880, three have names relating to the law:- "Judge", "Clerk" and "Defendant". Bloodhounds have always had a judicial look about them and they were used in an attempt to track the famous serial killer Jack the Ripper. It is not difficult to fathom the role of the Fox Terrier in society when names like "Butcher", "Racket", "Sergeant" and "Vigilant" are given even if one has to worry about the temperament of bitches given such names as "Vehement", "Volatile" and "Waspish". The Curly Coated Retriever bitch "Sweet Alice" reflected the delightful temperament that was already well developed in the retrievers.

The St. Bernard's association with monastic life is also reflected in the first registrations of this breed "Abbess IV", "Capuchin", "Pontiff" and what could be more appropriate than the dog registered as "Save". The list of interesting names seems almost endless with a total of about 4.7 million on record. Some sociologist of the future will find a rich vein to mine that will tell more about society's true feelings than any so called unbiased newspaper. But the sociologist will have to beware the occasional mistake that has crept in either through staff or printer error. Surely the Irish Terrier recorded as "Garlic" should have been registered as "Gaelic".

Another aspect of naming is the use of one particular word in conjunction with all the names of dogs bred by a particular kennel. These are correctly called affixes because they may be affixed to a dog's name either in front or at the back depending on the circumstances.

At first such words could be used either as a prefix or a suffix at the will of the owner. Later the rules were tightened up. The 1902 *Stud Book* was the first to list the affixes which had been granted. Today we have to publish them in a separate book because there are close to 60,000 of them. So famous have some of these affixes or "kennel names" become that they can be protected after the grantee is deceased. Many breed clubs do this so that important affixes in a breed will not be misused by someone else.

Not everyone was pleased at the idea of registration and the *Field* magazine started one of the great myths about the Kennel Club that reappears time after time. A money-making enterprise, they said, especially as there would be 100,000 registrations in a year. In the first month there were 165 registrations, and it was not until 1925 that the figure passed the 50,000 mark. The founder members of the Kennel Club were men of independent means and the registry was a follow-through on the fair play in competition idea which caused them to come together in the first place. It has always been the case that monies generated were and are ploughed back into dogs.

File Card record from 1913. One of over 2,000000 micro-filmed when computerisation was completed in 1983.

The First World War caused a major drop in the number of dogs being registered from 19,846 in 1913 to 3,383 in 1918. However, by 1921, the previous record had been broken with a total of over 23,000. The years leading up to the Second World War saw registrations reach over 57,000 but by the end of 1939 the figure was down to 36,124 and there were only 13,968 dogs registered in 1940. The low point came in 1941 with a figure of 12,467 but there is no doubt that the morale of the citizen in the United Kingdom was on the up and up after

this because the numbers of dogs being registered leapt dramatically: 21,073 in 1942; 35,359 in 1943; 53,563 in 1944 and 1945 saw registrations have a record year of 72,352.

Another interesting aspect of dogs that can be gathered from the registry is the proportion of sporting to non-sporting dogs. While many will deem the classification of dogs as arbitrary, dog people lump all the hounds, terriers and gundogs together as sporting dogs and the rest, including all the working dogs and the toys and others as non-sporting. The registration figures from 1908 show an almost equal balance of the two major groups but from 1914 onwards the scales tipped in favour of the sporting dog until by 1937 there were 41,000 sporting dogs registered to only 14,000 non-sporting. The years 1952 and 1953 recorded a reversal of this situation. If registration figures to the present day are followed with non-sporting going ahead for a number of years a balance has been gained again and we now see sporting dogs slightly in the lead.

Another of the common myths about the Kennel Club is that it is only interested in pedigree dogs. Registration records show that this has not been true at any time. History does prove, however, that the emphasis was on the pedigree dog until 1948 when what is now the Obedience and Working Trials Register began. The opportunity for the non-pedigree dog to compete in Kennel Club licensed competition could come about only if they were registered, a reiteration of the original reason for registration. It is possible to have a champion crossbred dog in Working Trials or Obedience.

What of the sheer physicality of keeping such records? For over 100 years each dog had its own filing card. The whole of the first floor at Clarges Street was dedicated to the storage of these cards. These cards were the back up system of those days. There were three records of any dog. One was the registration certificate that was sent to the owner. The second was the record published in the early days in the *Kennel Gazette* and latterly in the *Breed Record Supplement to The Stud Book* (to give its full title which is usually abbreviated to the BRS.). The third, up until 1983, was a filing card on the first floor. The filing card held a full history of the dog and was filed in alphabetical order of the dog's name within its breed. Apart from the breeder being recorded together with ownership and all transfers there were times when some show records were kept on the cards as well as results under the Kennel Club/British Veterinary Association health schemes results.

All systems can be improved and it was decided in 1976 to revamp the registration system with the creation of an impressive three tier system with all the appropriate paper work. A dog could be registered simply as a member of a litter. If this were the case each puppy in the litter was provided with a flimsy which could be used at a later date to register it either as a pet, with no check having been made of its proposed name, or as an actively registered dog that could compete in competition or could be used in a breeding programme. The system was as complicated as the last sentence! It meant that the paperwork for a dog might be handled three times even before any transfers.

The List of Fees that appears in each issue of the *Kennel Gazette* tells its own story as from April 1, 1976.

For all dogs born prior to April 1,1976 £3.00

For dogs born on or after April 1,1976:-
Litter Recording:-
Received within three months
from birth of litter £1.00
Received after three months
from birth of litter £5.00

Basic Registration by Breeder:-
Received within six months
from birth of dog £1.00
Received after six months
from birth of dog £2.50

Basic Registration by any person
other than Breeder £2.50

Registration in Active Register £1.50

If you are having trouble comprehending don't worry. So did the rest of the world of dogs. To say that the staff of the registration department were swamped is the understatement of the decade of the seventies. By 1978 it was realised that the system of registration had to be simplified. One tier, the basic, was taken out and ten years later a return was made to a single tier system. The trauma both in the office and among the breeders still shows its scars from time to time. You will still see the odd entry at a show with A.R.A.F. after its name. That stood for Active Registration Applied For and considering the change away from that system was in 1978 it shows how deeply traumatised we all were. Even the typing pool was frantic and I remember glancing

casually at a registration that was going out addressed to Mrs. H. M. Queen, Sandringham. Fortunately our patron did not receive that particular document but one wonders if there were any others that have caused a titter or two at teatime in the Palace.

1971 Registration Application signed by HM The Queen Mother and HM Queen Elizabeth II.

While the Kennel Club was the first with a registration system it was not the first to computerise. Some other Kennel Clubs had successfully made the transition but there were one or two spectacular failures. A former chairman of the Kennel Club, Leonard Pagliero, who is currently one of the Kennel Club vice-presidents, was the member who headed the drive to modernise the system. Everyone was wary but convinced that it was necessary or, as some said, it was a necessary evil. A Data General mainframe was installed in offices in Maidenhead and parallel systems were run for two years before the General Committee was happy that we could depend on the computer. The Kennel Club had to create its own programmes because there was nothing to be bought from the shelf and these tailormade programmes are themselves some of the less tangible treasures of the Kennel Club.

The old mainframe is now on its way and the club has invested in the latest technology to ensure that it can reap the maximum benefit

*1999 Litter Registration
Application Form.*

Change of name of a registered dog form.

from the system. The person who probably heaved the biggest sigh of relief when the full potential of the new technology was realised was the poor individual who typed the export pedigrees and the five generation pedigrees. There could be no alteration in these documents and if you made a mistake you had to go right back to the beginning and start again. An export pedigree is three generation and so there are 15 dogs' names which could be mistyped as well as the registration numbers. The biggest nightmare, however, was the five generation pedigree with 31 dogs' names and a mistake in the fifth generation could lead to suicide. There was a special typewriter reserved for the five generation pedigrees, the typeface of which was half the size of normal and so blindness was another hazard for the manual worker in the pre-computer era.

What of the future for this unique archive which houses information on the forebears of many countries' canine stock? The United Kingdom has created more breeds of dog than any other country and so the ancestral lines are in our registration records. All these records are based upon trust and there seems to be less trust about than there used to be.

Perhaps it was that we all had to trust one another's statements before but now there is the opportunity to check on parentage by DNA profiling. The Kennel Club already has the co-operation of the Southern Counties Staffordshire Bull Terrier Society in a pilot project for DNA profiling to validate registrations. Some of the older members will say it should not be necessary, but even the best breeders make the odd slip and with scientific benefits that can accrue in the identification of lines that carry hereditary diseases it would be criminal not to make the most of the most useful and important of the Treasures of the Kennel Club.

Brian Leonard

Library is a wealth of information

SINCE it was founded in 1873 the Kennel Club has acquired a wealth of information in the form of books, manuscripts, illustrations and memorabilia. Materials have come to the club in a haphazard fashion, partly as donations and partly as purchases. Archives of minutes and correspondence were scattered throughout the building, unrecorded and often hidden away in basements and cupboards.

In 1985 a huge step forward was made in the organisation of Kennel Club information and a library was established. This collection expanded rapidly and in 1989 a new air-conditioned library was built at Clarges Street, due mainly to the late chairman of the Kennel Club, John MacDougall, for insisting on the importance of books, for allocating space and for finally instigating the building of the library extension.

The Kennel Club library is now an international cynological resource, the largest of its kind in Europe, open to the public and providing space and atmosphere conducive to study and research. Situated on the ground floor of the building, it is easily accessible to all visitors. The collection covers every aspect of living with and keeping dogs. It endeavours to satisfy the ever increasing demand for canine information and to preserve information sources for the future. Its popularity has increased with improved awareness of its existence among the dog fraternity. Publicity in journals and newspapers, increased leaflet distribution, a stand at Crufts show and the autumn Discover Dogs at London's Earl's Court together with pages on the Internet have brought the library to the attention of interested parties at home and abroad.

The Kennel Club library's main objective is to provide and manage an information resource for Kennel Club members, Kennel Club staff and the general public, promoting in every way the general improvement of dogs. Rare materials are now only part of the library collection and the

services it has to offer. The library fulfils many roles as an archive, a museum, a picture library and a traditional reference library. It is staffed by two full-time professionals who answer enquiries in person, over the telephone or by post. In depth research and photocopying will also be undertaken for those who cannot visit.

The Library at Clarges Street was opened in November 1989 by HRH Prince Michael of Kent.

The library's book collection covers all canine matters. Its size is presently about 15,000 volumes. The earliest item Ulyssus Aldrovandus' *De Quadrupedib' digitatis vivipatris libri tres, et de quadrupedib' digitatis oviparis libri duo,* dates from 1637. Important new works are acquired as they come on to the market and over 100 donations are received each year. A computerised catalogue can be searched to find required items and subjects covered include history, care of the dog, breeding, training, sports and general breed books. The largest part of the collection is made up of materials, old and new, on the individual breeds, the oldest of which is *Observations on Prince Rupert's white dog, called Boy, 1642.* Boy was a poodle.

The library holds a considerable number of important and rare texts, one of the rarest being the *'Album of Northern Dogs'* by Prince Andrew Shirinski Shihmatoff Alexandrovitch, a former Associate Member of the Kennel Club. Its full Russian title is *Albom Sibirnish Sobaki (Laiki)* which translates as *Album of Northern Dogs*. The book was a private publication printed in 1896.

It is a strange book (or rather portfolio) partly in Russian and partly in English. It has a small inserted booklet in English which deals with the two major groups of Laikis. This work is the first important one to deal with Northern Dogs and the Kennel Club's copy was presented to S E Shirley, founder of the Kennel Club, by the author. The dedication leaf carries the holograph presentation inscription to Mr Shirley, ' in remembrance of his first visit to Moscow'.

Another recently acquired rare item was Christiano Francisco Paullini's *Cynographia Curiosa seu Canis Descriptio, Nuremburg 1685*. This is an important first edition with a rare woodcut frontispiece and is an exciting addition to the library. For its time, it provides an indepth insight into the physiology of dogs, the different breeds, and the classification, uses and management of dogs. It has little on British dogs but is believed to contain the first instance of the Dachshund being called by that name.

Various valuable scrap books and special collections have come into the hands of the Kennel Club, largely donated, or, occasionally, held by the library while still owned by individuals or clubs. As well as an insight into the lives of famous breeders and dog specialists, they are a comment on the social history of their respective times. The most important of the scrapbooks is that given to the Kennel Club by Lady Pentland. It is her grandfather, Lord Tweedmouth's *Stud Book and Inventory*. The first Lord Tweedmouth evolved one of the most popular breeds of today, the Golden Retriever. All his dogs, from 1835 onwards, are recorded and Golden Retrievers can be traced backwards, from the present day to the foundation of the breed. A small photograph at the front of the Tweedmouth Stud Book shows Lord Tweedmouth's keepers with his first Golden Retriever, Nous.

The largest scrapbook collection in the library is that which belonged to Mr Edwin Brough of Wyndyate, near Scarborough. He kept Bloodhounds and was referred to by A Croxton Smith as the 'greatest living authority on the breed' in an article in the *Windsor* magazine, 1895. Edwin Brough bred Bloodhounds throughout the latter part of the nineteenth century. He strengthened the breed in Britain at that time by bringing stock from France and by breeding stock with the strongest constitution to eliminate inherited weakness and produce vigorous and hardy offspring.

Mr Brough's scrapbooks, the earliest from 1865, outline a life devoted to his breed. They include correspondence, newspaper and journal articles from Britain and abroad, postcards, studcards and personal notes. Of particular interest are articles discussing Mr Brough's Bloodhounds involvement in attempts to catch the Whitechapel murderer known as Jack the Ripper. Mr Brough's painting of his dogs by Maud Earl, and a portrait of his dog Ch Bardoulph, by Rankin Poore are discussed elsewhere in the book.

Other notable scrapbooks include copies of H Reginald Cooke's *Scrapbooks on Flat Coated Retrievers*, papers from the Buccleuch Estate on Retrievers and papers belonging to Charles Cuthbert Eley on Terriers and Retrievers.

Items owned by the late Joan Bentley, Anne Argyle and Iain Gordon provide valuable information on English Toy Terriers, Whippets and Chihuahuas respectively. The Gwendoline Angel Collection on Salukis is heavily used for research. Other breeds covered by special collections include Irish Setters, English Setters, Clumber Spaniels, Boxers, Dachshunds, Pointers and King Charles Spaniels. A magnificent collection of trophies belonging to The Great Dane Club is on display in the library, and Kennel Club papers belonging to the Duke and Duchess of Windsor were

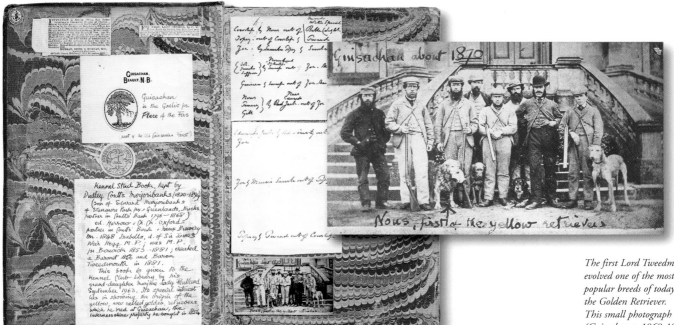

The first Lord Tweedmouth evolved one of the most popular breeds of today, the Golden Retriever. This small photograph (Guisachen c. 1868-1870) from the front of the Tweedmouth Stud Book shows James MacCallum, Head Gardner; Simon Munro, Head Keeper; Alex MacGillivary, Gamekeeper; Alex Munro, Handyman; Duncan MacLennan, Under Stalker; James Munro, Plumber; William Munro, Butler and James Cowan, Kennelman with Lord Tweedmouth's first Yellow Retriever, Nous, on the left.

purchased at the sale of their effects in New York in 1998.

Veronica Tudor Williams' extensive collection on the Basenji, which includes correspondence, photographs, slides and early pedigrees, is invaluable to researchers in this breed. The library holds copies of Veronica's four books, three entitled *Basenji: The Barkless Dogs,* and her book on her trip to Africa in search of Basenjis, *Fula: Basenji from the jungle.* Her collection includes the typescript of her first book *'Basenjis: The Barkless Dogs'* (privately printed by the author in 1946). The influence of Vernoica Tudor Williams on the Basenji is incalculable. During the second world war she persuaded the war-time Ministry of Food to allow her to obtain bomb-damaged food to feed her rare breed. In the 1950s she travelled to the Belgian Congo to obtain new stock. Throughout all, her dedication and commitment was without parallel. She brought a bitch puppy named Fula from the Congo in 1959 and American artist Andie Pasinger's tribute to Fula, her portrait, hangs in the library. Both Fula and her portrait are discussed in the chapter on the art collection.

The Kennel Club's own publications form the focus of many visiting researchers work. A complete set of *Kennel Club Stud Books,* from 1873, and *Kennel Club Breed Record Supplements* are available. The *Kennel Gazette* is held in hard copy beginning with its first issue

of 1880. Recent years are also held on CD-ROM improving access to the information it holds. The minutes of all Kennel Club Committee and sub-committees are stored in the library and permission can be sought to view these. Other valuable official publications are those from Kennel Clubs abroad. The *American Kennel Club Stud Book,* the Japanese and some European stud books are available.

Many breed club year books and bulletins can be found and supplement the collection with detailed information on pedigrees and breeders not always available in commercially published books. Articles from all the British national newspapers are stored chronologically within subject areas. These cover all canine matters. Copies of the weekly newspaper *Dog World* are held from 1984 onwards, *Our Dogs* from 1926. British, European, American and Australian canine journals support topics covered by the book stock. Information sheets on each breed of dog recognised by the Kennel Club are available from the library for those requiring brief information. They give photographs of the breeds, details from the Kennel Club breed standards, breed club contacts and books to read. Most championship show catalogues, marked with results, are held. The earliest catalogue is from 1869, the earliest Crufts catalogue from 1891.

The Kennel Club picture library has doubled in recent years and now houses approximately

The library's automated catalogue can be used to search for books. Other databases and the Internet can also be accessed.

15,000 photographs and illustrations. It is managed separately from the library's reference collections as images are lent to individuals, publishers and the media for reproduction. Library staff are involved in all Kennel Club projects involving illustrations, for instance the production of the Kennel Club calendars and the publication of the successful reference book, *The Kennel Club's Illustrated Breed Standards.*

The objective of the Kennel Club is to promote, in every way, the general improvement of dogs. With this in mind the picture library aims to provide photographs and illustrations showing positive images of the dog, both from the present day and the past. Subjects covered include adult dogs and puppies, care and training, showing and other activities, country sports, personalities and the Royal Family with their dogs. In many instances, images of events of the past not only show changes in the breeds, but also offer an insight into social history. They show those involved in events, often offering excellent portrayals of respected judges, breeders, Kennel Club members and the Royal Family actively engaged in the pursuits they most enjoy with their dogs.

Crufts, the world's greatest dog show, provides a spectacular subject for photographers. The Kennel Club's picture library covers every aspect of this event today, as well as depicting the Crufts shows of the past. Numerous other championship shows are covered, and of particular note are early scenes of such as the Ladies Kennel Association show. The picture library represents the work of many different photographers and new stock is continually added. High quality prints and transparencies are available for reproduction immediately at reasonable rates, as is film footage from Crufts.

The Kennel Club art collection, as discussed in this book, is managed by the library staff and copy prints of the art can be purchased through the library. Art work, from magazines and journals from the late nineteenth and early twentieth centuries, is also held.

The Kennel Club library continues to grow in size, and improve in terms of information provided with ease of access to that information. The collection is invaluable, and as a diverse resource, encompassing many media, it is absolutely unique. It satisfies the research needs of hundreds of customers each year, and fascinates all who enter its door. It also supports the staff of the Kennel Club in their endeavours to provide a service to all customers, and the organisation as a whole in its promotion of the general improvement of dogs.

Barbara Walker

History shows how kings and queens have loved dogs

OVER *the years kings and queens* have shown their love of dogs and their interest in certain breeds as pets, working dogs or presents. The famous Mastiffs of Lyme Park were presented as gifts from James I to the Kings of Spain and Denmark.

Henry VIII, better known to history for his wives, mentions in his Privy Purse expenses "Cut the King's spanyelle." Charles II's Court was filled with small spaniels and later one of the spaniel breeds was to take his name.

The fated Stuarts were great dog lovers. Prince Rupert's famous Poodle, Boye, killed at the battle of Marston Moor, was supposed to have been adept at catching Parliamentary bullets in his mouth.

Mary Queen of Scots' beloved dog was with her on the scaffold and afterwards would not leave the corpse. James I bought terriers from Scotland when he came to England as King. William and Mary had Pugs. The famous dog collar presented by Alexander Pope to George II when he was Prince of Wales, said *I am His Highness Dog at Kew; Pray tell me Sir, whose dog are you?*

But the first monarch not only to keep many dogs but to show and win was Queen Victoria. Her kennels were in Home Park, Windsor, and the Queen's verandah was where she would sit and view the dogs' paddock and the apron piece where the dogs were brought for her to see. In her room in the cottage were the Queen's albums of dog portraits as far back as 1845. Queen Victoria had a great variety of dogs, some given by overseas dignatories, such as the Cashmere dog, a Chusan Chow, Cuba dogs, Esquimaux dog, Russian Greyhound, Black Pug, White Collies, and a Chinese Spaniel.

Queen Victoria named the dogs herself and over the years tended to use the same names. In this room at the cottage were trophies and medals won by the Windsor dogs when shown: a silver cup won by the Collie Darnley for best local exhibit at Crufts; a beaker awarded to Fluffy the Spitz who won wherever shown; the Pomeranians won the Kennel Club medal in 1873, the Crystal Palace Breeders medal, Crufts Gold medal for the best team of Pomeranians (Fluffy, Beppo and Alfeo) and the Pomeranian Club's two gold and silver medals; there was also the Skye Terrier Diana of Aldevalloch's gold medal from the Skye Club of Scotland.

Special presentation catalogues of the shows were presented to the Queen.

In the Green Room the Queen had framed the prize certificates won by her dogs at Islington and the Crystal Palace. Hugh Brown, younger brother of John Brown, Queen Victoria's famous Highland ghillie was, before he went to New Zealand, head kennelman and he was succeeded by Joseph Hill who trained on the Collie farm of Mr. Samuel Boddington, breeder of the great Champion Rutland.

The Queen's Dachshunds were given to her by relatives in Germany and all her dogs were of high quality. Two Irish Terriers, Paddy and Biddy, were presented and bred by Mr. G. Krehl. Paddy, by Terrian Boy ex Sheuhte Agra and born September 1890, was a good specimen who won 1st at Uxbridge before joining the Windsor Kennel.

The Queen also had a great interest in Greyhounds and Deerhounds and names and particulars are entered in the Windsor Register.

The Rev Thomas Pearce, better known as "Idstone" a prolific writer for *Field,* tells us that the Deerhounds at Windsor were highly esteemed by Prince Albert and the Queen. Four of them were exhibited at Islington in 1869 by John Cole, for many years head keeper at Windsor, and the best of all the exhibits at the show were Hubert, Caird and Mink.

In Cassell's *Book of the Dog* it states that John Cole owned several splendid Deerhounds bred from Prince Albert's Hector. From the Prince's

Bran was descended Torrum, the grandsire of Gillespies' famous Torrum. Queen Victoria, much to Charles Cruft's great delight, often exhibited at Crufts show but, after an outbreak of distemper in her kennels (which the Queen thought they had caught at a show), she never exhibited again.

The year 1892 was a great one for Crufts and royalty. The Czar of Russia sent six Borzois. Queen Victoria exhibited Poms, a Skye Terrier and a Collie. The Princess of Wales showed a St. Bernard and a Basset Hound while the Prince of Wales showed a terrier. The Queen kept many dogs in the home kennels at Windsor and when she died there were 83 there. She died at Osborne in the Isle of Wight and her favourite black Pomeranian lay on the end of her bed.

King Edward VII with Caesar his dog, c. 1908

In 1875 the Prince of Wales became patron of the Kennel Club and continued in this office after his accession to the throne as Edward VII. It was his backing for the abolition of cropping dogs' ears that helped to make it illegal. Before the founding of the Kennel Club in 1873 the Prince of Wales, as he then was, won with his harrier at the Second International Dog Show at Islington.

In Charles Lane's *Dog Show and Doggy People,* King Edward VII is pictured at Balmoral in September, 1899, with a French Bulldog, Peter, imported from France, whose son Paul won a second prize at the Bulldog Club Show in 1901. The King introduced Clumber Spaniels to Sandringham for working and he also showed them. Sandringham Lucy, bred by the King, won a third prize at Crufts.

In 1907, at Manchester Championship Show, Sandringham Lucy won the challenge certificate. The King's last dog was his beloved pet Fox Terrier, Caesar, bred by the Duchess of Newcastle and thus "bred in the purple". His pedigree name was Caesar of Notts. When the King died the dog was inconsolable and walked in the funeral procession beside the King's charger, led by Maclean the Royal ghillie and gun loader. Caesar is immortalized on the tomb of Edward VII in St. George's Chapel, Windsor.

At the foot of the effigy of the King lies the white marble figure of Caesar, curled in sleep.

Queen Alexandra had always been interested in dogs since her childhood as a Danish princess. She was very involved in the breeding and showing of her dogs. Sandringham was her favourite country house and Edward VII closed the kennels at Windsor and his late mother's dogs were all moved there. In 1897 an article in the *Ladies Kennel Journal* tells us that at Sandringham there were 70 dogs (not counting the dogs kept for sporting purposes). The Royal kennels were said to be as fine as the Royal stables, well ventilated and fitted with hot water pipes, paddocks, inside yards, kitchen, hospital and puppy room.

Queen Alexandra was patron of the Ladies' Kennel Association. One breed with which she is indelibly linked is the Borzoi or Russian Wolfhound. One of the best known of her dogs was Alex, given to her by her brother-in-law, Tsar Alexander II of Russia. Alex became a champion when the Queen was still Princess of Wales. He won over 100 awards, including the 500 guinea Dohlpur Gold Cup in 1910. People would queue at shows to see this famous Royal dog. She made up another champion in Champion Vassilica when she became Queen and also exhibited Basset Hounds. Her first, Babil and Bijan, were given to her by the Comtesse de Paris and both were prize winners. Queen Alexandra built up an important kennel, in Roughs, exhibiting Ch. Sandringham Bobs, Ch. Sandringham Vanity, Ch. Sandringham Valour and Ch. Sandringham Valens.

His Majesty King George V's Labrador Retrievers in 1935.

In Basset Hounds, Smooth, were Ch. Sandringham Dido, Ch. Sandringham Warrender and Ch. Sandringham Weaver. Her son King George V, used the affix Wolferton (a village on the Sandringham Estate) while she was alive but after the death of his mother on November 20, 1925, took over the Sandringham prefix.

In 1916 George V won a first at Crufts with his three-year-old Laborador bitch, Wolferton Jet, who went on to win the Kennel Club challenge certificate at Manchester that year. She was the dam of Wolferton Dan, CC winner at the Scottish Kennel Club in 1923. Dan sired the successful Sh.Ch. Wolferton Sheila, winner of five CCs, including Crufts. At the then Sandy Championship Show the King did the "double" with Wolferton Ben and Sheila.

In 1923, Wolferton Solo, bred by Lord Knutsford and litter sister to Ch. Banchory Danilo came to Sandringham as already a good winner. Although the Labradors were used on the Royal shoots and King George V was a famous shot, it seems none were entered to gain the certificate which would make them a full champion.

Clumber Spaniels were also reintroduced and Thomas Fall's photographs show some very handsome specimens of the breed. At Crufts in 1934 Sandringham Spark (by Sandringham Sport ex Sandringham Speck) won a second and a third prize. He had also won at Crufts in 1932.

King George V died on January 20, 1936, to be succeeded by King Edward VIII, later to become the Duke of Windsor on his abdication. He had first shown Gwen, a Welsh Terrier at the Kennel Club Show at the Crystal Palace in 1912. She won first prize but did not carry on a show career. One of the best known winners of the then Prince of Wales was the Alsatian, Claus of Seale who won for the Prince a challenge certificate and many other awards. The Prince did not show his Cairn Terriers but after the abdication the Duke and Duchess of Windsor showed their Pugs in America and Europe and won high honours with Goldengleam Trooper and PugVilles Imperial II.

The youngest son of George V, the Duke of Kent, when he was H.R.H. Prince George, showed the lovely Great Dane Ch. Midas of Send. He also owned the beautifully-bred Chow, Choonam Li Wu T'Song, said to be very much the favourite of the present Princess Alexandra when she was a child. The Chow's pet name was Muff.

The fourth son of George V to be involved with show dogs was the Duke of Gloucester with his wife, later H.R.H. Princess Alice, Duchess of Gloucester. They probably had the greatest influence on a breed of all the Royal

Family. That breed was the Australian Terrier. The Duke brought two back from Australia after a visit in 1934. In 1945 the Duke became Governor General of Australia and while there once more had Australian Terriers. When they returned to Britain in 1947 they brought their two dogs with them, bred from the best lines in Australia, Kursaal Blue Piper and Kursaal Blue Jean.

A litter was bred from Jean by Ch. Dunhall Wrastel. A bitch from the litter, shown by the owner of the sire, Mrs. Dunn, became Ch. Dunhall Wroyal Blue and won the challenge certificate at Crufts in 1955 and 1956 and she became the dam of champions.

Edward VIII with a Pug, 'The Imp', at a show in Deauville, USA, July 1959.

The mating was repeated and this time Mrs. Dunn had a dog who became Champion Dunhall Blue Wroyalist. He was a significant sire lying behind the influential Spenmoss kennel. Princess Alice bred on her line, always trying to keep her Australian terriers as 'Australian' as it was possible using, when able, imported bloodlines. She was knowledgeable about the breed and the last of Princess Alice's Australian Terriers was buried in the dog cemetery at Barnwell Manor in 1978.

King George VI was most interested in the training of his Labradors for shooting and in 1939 the black Labrador, Sandringham Stream, won the cup for the best gundog at the Kings Lynn show. One of the kennel's great field trial achievements was to win the Kennel Club's open retriever trial (a two-day stake) at Sutton Scotney, Hampshire, on November 4 and 5 1948 with Windsor Bob, owned by the King, bred and handled by George Hallett, the head keeper at Windsor (by Dual Champion Staindrop Saighdear ex F.T.Ch. Braeroy Fudge), King George VI died in February, 1953.

Queen Elizabeth II had her own original Pembroke Welsh Corgi from her father, King George VI, although she had grown up with the special companionship of the family's Corgis. Susan, from kennels in Cambridgeshire, was given to her in 1944 as her own dog, registered name Hickathrift Pippa. Although she was not shown, the Queen, using outside stud dogs, now has Corgis in about the tenth generation directly descended from Susan. It can be seen

HM The Queen and members of the Royal Family at Balmoral, September 1979, with their dogs.

from photographs and television just how typical they are. The Corgis use the prefix Windsor and Her Majesty is as keenly interested in the breeding of her dogs as she is in the breeding of her horses.

The Queen has also built up a kennel of Labradors with the emphasis on working ability. The Duke of Edinburgh bred Sandringham Mint, who won two novice stakes in 1956 and went on to win a certificate of merit in open stakes.

Mint's grandchildren include FT.Ch. Sandringham Ranger and others who won well. Sherry of Biteabout was bought in at six weeks old and in time she too became a field trial Champion. Bill Meldrum, the Queen's head keeper at Sandringham at that time said Mint was a lovely bitch to handle and that the Queen enjoyed handling her on the Royal shoots. FT.Ch. Sandringham Slipper was something special and achieved her title in ten days, progressing the hard way from novice to champion status. She was also fourth in the prestigious Retriever Championship in 1968 and second in 1969.

The Queen's Labrador which was known, it seemed, by everybody was FT.Ch. Sandringham Sydney. He was the star of a television documentary about the Royal Labradors in 1977 called *Sandringham Sydney and Co.* Sydney sired FT.Ch. Sandringham Salt who gained his title in 1982.

All the dogs at Sandringham are there basically as shooting dogs for the Royal family and in addition to the Labradors there are usually a few working English Springers and Cocker Spaniels.

Her Majesty very much 'runs' her kennel. She decides which bitches are to be mated to whom and when they shall be bred from. She names all her dogs and those in the Norfolk Kennel all use the Sandringham prefix.

Some puppies are sold to working homes and FT.Ch. Sandringham Magpie and FT.Ch. Sandringham Moccasin were two which were made up. The Queen is known as a good handler and has taken great interest in field trials and has on occasion judged at trials.

She regularly gives permission for trials at Sandringham, not least among them the Kennel Club's own trials. Her Majesty is patron of the Kennel Club while its president is H.R.H. Prince Michael of Kent, who also has Labradors.

Continuing a Royal tradition, there was an entry in the 1997 Crufts Clumber Spaniel special field trial bitch class of a bitch, Tinglestone Spot Scherzando, which had been bred in 1992 by The Princess Royal, whose home is at Gatcombe Park, Gloucestershire.

The Queen has a world-famed collection of paintings and among these are those by famous artists depicting Royal pets.

Queen Victoria was especially fond of Sir Edwin Landseer and Gourley Steele. One of Landseer's most successful dog portraits was *Windsor Castle in Modern Times* in which Prince Albert has just returned from hunting. A portrait of Princess Alice and Dandy, the Skye Terrier, was a birthday present to Queen Victoria.

Queen Victoria was often the first to have new breeds. *Minka and Bent* shows a Tibetan Mastiff. There is also the Friedrich Wilhelm Keyl picture of Lootie, brought to England from Peking, one of the first Pekingese into the country. Among others are the superb picture by Sir Samuel Luke of Queen Alexandra, when Princess of Wales, portrayed with one of her favourite Japanese Chins; a rare Thomas Blinks; a Fred Morgan of Queen Alexandra with her grandchildren and her favourite pets. Reuben Ward Binks created some lovely paintings of the King George V Clumbers. One must conclude that there must be many more paintings of Royal dogs which have never been seen or known to us.

Valerie Foss

Crufts is synonymous with excellence

"*DOG shows preceded* field trials by six years," wrote E. W. Jaquet, secretary of the Kennel Club and author of the famous record of the history and work of the club in the years from its founding in 1873 to 1905.

He goes on to tell us that on February 2, 1869, an organisation called the National Dog Club was started, whose first and only show was in June of the same year. Financially it was a disaster and the club practically collapsed following it.

Owing to the risk involved it was not easy to form a committee to run another show in or near London but, eventually, arrangements were made to run one at the Crystal Palace in June, 1870, termed *The First Grand Exhibition of Sporting and Other Dogs.* The show, says Jaquet, was a good one but "financially was a failure" and the committee headed by Mr. S. E. Shirley and Mr. J. H. Hutchison, had to bear a heavy loss.

So bad were things that the next year several members of the committee declined to be involved, but a second exhibition of dogs **was** held, with a much smaller deficit. The inconvenience of organising a fresh committee each year, lack of permanent staff, no funds, no regular office (meetings were in the British Hotel, Cockspur Street) and other associated problems began to take their toll.

And so it came that Mr. Shirley founded the Kennel Club, with the first meeting in April, 1873. Thus established, the Kennel Club's own first show took place at the Crystal Palace, Sydenham, on four days - June 17, 18, 19 and 20, 1873. There 975 entries. One year later the show was not just under Kennel Club patronage but also under the rules and management of the club.

The 1873 catalogue listed 24 members of the Kennel Club of whom nine were members of the committee and identified at the show by the "silver crosses with crimson ribbons" which they wore.

If divine protection were deemed necessary at least it was spread to the judges, manager and secretary, all of whom wore similar crosses, with each category wearing a different coloured ribbon.

The catalogue of this show was highly prized, as is evidenced by the copy in the Kennel Club library. This copy had been presented to The Bulldog Club (Inc.) by Sam Woodiwiss at the end of his year of office as president in December, 1917. It was presented to the Kennel Club in 1988 by the Bulldog Club.

But let it not be thought that the Kennel Club had just one show in those days. In 1878 there was one show at the Crystal Palace and another at Alexandra Palace. In 1879 there were two shows, one at Alexandra Palace and one at Brighton. The first issue of the *Kennel Gazette* in 1880 stated that "the Kennel Club show will be held in the north end of the Crystal Palace, on a level with the main part of the building."

It is possible to determine from this that the show was not in the famous palace itself but was an outdoor show. The Crystal Palace was built for the 1851 Exhibition in Hyde Park and then moved to the site in Sydenham.

The Kennel Club continued to run its own show, building it up little by little. A typical catalogue is that for the 1925 show. There were 2123 dogs entered. Francis Redmond was one of the guarantors and when one reads that his address was Whetstone House, Totteridge,

The Kennel Club Dog Show at the Crystal Palace. From the top, and from left to right, the Prince of Wales' Rough-Coated Basset Hound, Beauty II; the Prince of Wales' Basset Hound, Bonnie II; Mr. C. C. Haldenby's Foreign Dog, Fanica; Mr. O. C. Thompson's Poodle, King II; Mr. George R. Sims' Dalmatian, Samson and Mr. Brough's Bloodhound, Brunhilda. Illustration by Cecil Aldin taken from the London Illustrated News, Nov. 3 1894.

CHOW · BORZOI · NEWFOUNDLAND · MASTIFF · IRISH WATER SPANIEL · COLLIE · FOXHOUND · GREYHOUND · IRISH WOLFHOUND · POODLE · BLOODHOUND · AFGHAN GREYHOUND · ENGLISH SETTER · DALMATIAN · DEERHOUND · POINTER

Types of dogs at the show in the Agricultural Hall. Crufts 10-12 February 1910. Taken from The Graphic, 12th February 1910.

London N20, a light dawns. The title for one of his best-known works of canine art was *The Totteridge Eleven* (described in the chapter on paintings).

This same catalogue shows us that there already existed a good working relationship with a certain Charles Cruft, a man who had vision and the talents to develop canine exhibitions shortly after leaving college in 1876. He had gone to work for James Spratt in Holborn, selling Spratt's famous "dog cakes". As he travelled the country he visited large estates and sporting kennels and later his career took him to France and, in 1878, French dog breeders invited him to organise and promote the canine section of the Paris Exhibition.

He took up the management in 1886 of the Allied Terrier Club Show at the Royal Aquarium, Westminster, and in 1891 promoted the first show in his own name at the Royal Agricultural Hall, Islington.

Charles Cruft had a long and extremely successful career organising his dog shows, but he died in 1938, leaving his widow to run the 1939 Crufts show. Mrs. Cruft found the

responsibility too demanding and approached the Kennel Club to perpetuate the show her husband had made famous. She stipulated in the contract of sale that the name of its founder, Charles Cruft, remained.

Of course, the Kennel Club had continued to run its own shows but with the acquisition of Crufts show the Kennel Club Show disappeared as a primary title. One of the consequences of this has been that many outside the immediate show world and, indeed, many overseas visitors, do not realise that Crufts is the Kennel Club show.

Perhaps Charles would have a quiet giggle that his name was perpetuated, and will be as long as dog shows exist, at the expense of the Kennel Club, his old rival.

There is no doubt that the Kennel Club has gained. No other show in the world is as big. No other show in the world attracts the media in the same numbers.

The word "Crufts" is synonymous with excellence and quality and there is no doubt, either, that the importance of the Kennel Club Show, which has been replaced by Crufts, now run by the Kennel Club, gives the Kennel Club a great opportunity to communicate the concerns of the world of dogs to the widest possible audience. And that is what makes it a treasure of the Kennel Club.

Before 1928 Crufts did not have an award of "best in show". Since 1929 there have been 62 best in show winners at Crufts, excluding the year in which this book is published. The first was a Greyhound, Primely Sceptre, owned by H. Whitley, and this has been followed by a succession of famous names across a variety of breeds.

Several breeds have been represented more than once in the honours list but perhaps the most significant sequence was a series of Cocker Spaniels carrying the affix *"of Ware"*.

All owned and exhibited by H. S. Lloyd, there was Lucky Star of Ware in 1930 and 1931, Exquisite Model of Ware in 1938 and 1939 and then, after a nine-year gap because of the Second World War, Tracy Witch of Ware in 1948 and 1950, the 1949 show having been cancelled.

For years the Kennel Club had put on Crufts at Olympia but pressure on space saw the show

The finalists for best in show, Crufts 1999, parade into the main ring and stand in the spotlights, watched by the judge (centre right).

Crufts 1999, Best in Show, Irish Setter Sh Ch Caspians Intrepid with owner Jackie Lorrimer, and
Reserve Best in Show, David Killilea's Japanese Akita, Ch Redwitch Dancin' in the Dark. Pictured with them Mrs Liz Cartledge (BIS judge),
the Earl of Buchan, a vice-president of the Kennel Club, who presented the awards, and Miss Sybil Churchill, chairman of Crufts.

111

Sir Dudley Forwood Bart
Chairman of Crufts 1973-1987

M. J. R. Stockman MRCVS
Chairman of Crufts 1989-1992

Mark Hutchings (left) Chairman of Crufts
1993-1996 with Tony Blunt (Hearing Dogs for
the Deaf) and Sue Longridge (Sherleys).

Wing Cmdr
W. A. 'Jimmy' Iles,
Chairman of Crufts 1988

Miss M. S. Churchill
Chairman of Crufts
1997-present pictured
with Finnish judge
Rainer Vuorinen.

move to Earls Court in 1979. Increasing entries had the show bursting at the seams and in 1982 the show was extended to three days while in 1987 it expanded to four. Still numbers rose, both of entries and spectators, and many will recall the "log jams" which took place in those last years at Earls Court.

In 1991 the show moved out of London for the first time in its history and celebrated the Crufts centenary at the Birmingham National Exhibition Centre. Each succeeding show at the NEC has seen further growth, change and expansion.

There is no doubt that if Charles Cruft were still alive he would be extremely proud of the way in which his show has been managed and developed.

It is probably true to say that it was under the chairmanship of Sir Dudley Forwood that the first changes came about to make the show what it is today. There is little doubt that as it moves into the new millennium further developments will alter its character and size.

Sir Dudley was a good chairman of Crufts. He was a member of the General Committee and thus privy to all that went on behind the scenes. He had a charm and personality which exuded *bon homie*. He had connections which aided him in his role and, above all, though not a man to tolerate fools gladly, led a team which put on a good show.

He was followed in office by Wing Cmdr WAJ ("Jimmy") Iles, Mike Stockman, Mark Hutchings and, currently, Miss Sybil Churchill, all prominent Kennel Club and General Committee members.

Each has stamped their individual mark on the show but under, firstly, Mark Hutchings and, latterly, Miss Churchill audiences around the world have seen its television coverage blossom into a colourful spectacle, giving it the sense of occasion which not even Charles Cruft managed to achieve.

Crufts is Crufts. There is nothing quite like it anywhere in the world and ... it is still the Kennel Club Show!

Brian Leonard and
Bernard Hall

Trialling has changed little since 1865

KENNEL Club field trials are highly regarded among the gundog fraternity and rightly so for they have a long history. The first trial under Kennel Club rules was in September 1873, some five months after the club was founded. It was held at Orwell Park, Ipswich, on the estate of Col Tomline, MP, and, as in so many instances of first-time Kennel Club events, the club's founder, Sewallis Evelyn Shirley, was among the judges.

But this was not the first field trial ever held. The first trial of dogs in the field was on Tuesday, April 18, 1865, at Southill, Bedfordshire, over the estate of Mr Samuel Whitbread, MP, and was for Pointers and Setters. The order of procedure was not so vastly dissimilar to what happens today, except that awards were given in accordance with a scale of points, interestingly divided as follow: Nose 40 points; pace and range, 30; temperament, 10; staunchness before 10, behind, 10. Style, of course was also taken into consideration. Today, in all trials be they for Pointers and Setters, Retrievers, Spaniels or Hunt Point and Retrieve breeds, the judges are advised by Kennel Club rules to place dogs in a category such as A, B or C (+ or -) according to the work done.

The second trials were held at Cannock Chase, Stafford, in 1866 and, a year later, there were two meetings, namely the National Pointer and Setter Trials at Stafford and the first field trials on partridge at Bala, North Wales. In 1868 the only recorded trial was the National Pointer and Setter, again at Stafford.

In 1870 there were three meetings, at Southampton, Shrewsbury and Bangor. Shrewsbury had been a venue the year before also. There were a further three in 1871, the first two as in 1870 but the Bangor trial was dropped and Vaynol was substituted as the venue. By 1872 there were four fixtures, the new ground being Menheniot, Cornwall.

This was the first time any trial had been held in the West Country, let alone Cornwall.

Then we come to the first Kennel Club trial, at Orwell Park, where, though other venues were selected in following years, Col Tomline's successor at Orwell, Mr E G Pretyman, placed the estate at the disposal of the Kennel Club for 11 years up to 1905. The second Kennel Club field trial was held on the estate of the Marquess of Bristol at Sleaford, Lincolnshire, in 1874. The field trials of 1875 are memorable as in that year began the long series of Kennel Club field trial Derbys, still carried on today. The 1999 Champion Stake for Pointers and Setters included in the qualification for entry "the winner of the 1998 Champion Stake and the winner of the Kennel Club Derby Stake, 1999."

General view taken at a Pointer and Setter stake with competitors waiting to go into line.

Though in the early days Kennel Club trials were based on Pointers and Setters, as the years passed trials were offered for Retrievers, Spaniels and, since the growth of interest in the hunt, point and retrieve breeds arriving here from Europe, for these as well.

From the earliest of trials to the present time there have been and are problems over the manner in which trials are organised, run and judged, needing constant supervision of and change to the rules by which they are governed. Field trial rules as at first drafted in 1874 remained unaltered until October, 1879.

113

A German Short-Haired Pointer, one of the hunt, point and retrieve breeds at work in a Kennel Club trial.

The line waits in a retriever trial while dog No. 23 works out in sugar beet.

E W Jaquet writes in his esteemed work on the history of the Kennel Club, "The way of the transgressor, during the continuance of the unrevised Field Trial Rules, was hard, for Rule 5, which dealt with defaulters, enacted 'that no person shall be allowed to enter or run a dog in his own or any other person's name who is a defaulter for either entries or stakes, in field trials, dog shows, racing or coursing meetings'."

There was also a rule which related to the practice of betting, "a proceeding which was probably equally distasteful to 'the sportsmen' who in the past were debarred by the clause relating to entries and stakes in relation to racing and coursing."

Kennel Club trophies on offer to the winner of the club's two-day open retriever trial.

Defaulting on a bet needed a complaint to be lodged with the secretary of the Kennel Club within six months of payment becoming due and, "if the bet was not paid or the person against whom the claim was made did not appear before the Kennel Club at the next meeting after receiving notice to do so and successfully

resist the claim," he was considered a defaulter. The portion of the rule relating to bets was retained until 1890 when the Field Trial Rules were again revised.

So. through the years trials have grown and, since the Second World War, there has been an explosion in the number of persons running in field trials. In their early days triallers were mainly from the large estates up and down the country but today one finds more triallers from the ranks of ordinary folk, both town and country, enjoying a sport which has existed in Britain for well over 130 years and which grew out of man's innate desire to hunt.

In the 1999/2000 season the major Kennel Club retriever and spaniel trials were organised as follow: Retriever (24 dog) open stake at Plas Nantyr, Llangollen, Wales; Retriever (16 dog) novice stake at Stody, near Holt, Norfolk; Cocker Spaniel (18 dog) open and the Any Variety Spaniel, except Cockers, (18 dog) both at Ulverton, Cumbria.

The previous season saw the Kennel Club run two trials in Northern Ireland and one in Scotland, following the pattern of recent years to move around the British Isles.

The Kennel Club also runs its trials for Pointers and Setters. The P and S Spring Trials in 1999 were held at Six Mile Bottom, as they have been for many years, although the trials for 1998 had to be cancelled because of the rapid and high growth of the wheat on the ground.

Hunt, point and retrieve breeds currently have a trial run by the Kennel Club every other year. This alternates with the HPR Championship.

The trophy for the winner of the Kennel Club gundog working test.

Gundog Working Tests

In 1946 the first gundog working test was devised by the United Retriever Club as an aid to training. Over the years its popularity has grown as a competition until now hundreds of tests are run each year, organised by a variety of gundog clubs.

In 1997 members of the Kennel Club field trials sub-committee felt it was wrong that such a well-supported sport, already run under Kennel Club regulations, was not an event which the Kennel Club itself organised. Within the year the first Kennel Club gundog working test, for retrievers which had won in some of the country's prestigious tests, was held at Tatton Park, Knutsford, Cheshire. It proved to be a great success and had the support of the National Gundog Association, who presented the runner-up trophy.

In 1998 a second test was run, again at Tatton Park and, equally was successful but, ironically as the ground offered on this huge estate was restricted and it was hoped to introduce Spaniels in its third year, the decision was made to move the event for 2000 to Arbury Park, near Nuneaton. It appears that this will become an annual fixture and another "treasure" of the Kennel Club.

WORKING TRIALS

The first Kennel Club working trials were at Enfield on October 25, 1975. This may come as a surprise to some for one tends to think that working trials have been around for years.

Of course, they have, but the Kennel Club *Year Book* of 1976, in its summary of events for the previous year states: "The highlight of working trials activities in 1975 was the scheduling of the First Kennel Club Working Trials Championships (at Enfield)".

It had been decided that these championships should be organised by a Kennel Club registered society and the Associated Sheep, Police and Army Dog Society (ASPADS) was selected to conduct the first championships. Tracking dog and police dog stakes were held under Mr J Cree and Mr J Dykes respectively.

The *Year Book* adds: "The championships were well organised and highly appreciated by all connected with working trials and will henceforth be an important event in the Kennel Club calendar."

For the record, the TD stake was won by Mrs S Hodson's Labrador WT Ch Linnifold Black Magic and Police Con Lake's Alsatian (GSD) Bois of Limbrook, an experienced police dog, was the winner of the PD championship.

Turning the pages back we find that working trials had, indeed, been in operation for many years before the Kennel Club took them under its wing. In 1926, nearly 50 years earlier, the Bi-Annual Meeting of the Kennel Club passed rules and regulations for Alsatian Wolf Dog Working Trials, which had originally been drafted by a special committee.

By 1935 a resolution was being sent to the General Committee asking the Kennel Club to recognise officially the qualifications gained at championship working trials by allowing such qualifications to appear and remain on export pedigrees and in the *Kennel Club Stud Book* and in registrations

The General Committee duly considered this and pointed out that working trial winners were duly recorded in the *Stud Book* and the title of champion would be attached to all official documents, providing the same information for working trial winners as for for field trial winners.

Bloodhound Trials

The first field trials for Bloodhounds were held in October, 1898, a year after the founding of the Association of Bloodhound Breeders, but most owners in those early days were more interested in the show ring than working their hounds and so support for trials was slow. Even so the first Kennel Club field trial championship certificate was awarded in 1900.

During the First World War trials were halted (in 1918) and resumed in 1922. This restart saw a swing of enthusiasm for work away from shows. The Second World War was more serious and it was only through a handful of members that there was continuity of both the breed and the association, enabling field trials to recommence in 1950.

OBEDIENCE

The Kennel Club obedience championship was born out of displays put on at Crufts. An innovation at the 1952 show was the display which took place each day in a large ring in the National Hall, Olympia. The competing dogs had been selected from principal winners in obedience tests "C" at the 1951 series of obedience shows.

This agility competitor already has his eye on the next obstacle.

For the public the display proved to be a major attraction and the ringside and the overhead gallery were filled with spectators throughout judging by Mr George Sly, who even tried tempting dogs to move from their sit or stay positions by offering them meat.

The obedience display presented in the National Hall in 1953 again attracted a vast audience. It was planned that the first obedience

Mary Ray working one of her dogs in the Crufts obedience ring.

championship show run by the Kennel Club should be in 1954 but it was not as the whole show was cancelled. The first Kennel Club championship obedience event was finally held in 1955 and it was again Mr George Sly who was the judge.

The bitch winner was Mr W J Spencer's Alsatian, Ob Ch Della of Gipton and the dog winner, Miss Dorothy Homan's Alsatian, Sheperdon Spun Gold.

Since those days obedience has continued to take its place at Crufts and today is still watched by large audiences .

AGILITY

John Varley, a former member of the Crufts Committee, was looking for demonstrations to interest the ringside audience and he related this need to his experiences with the horse jumping world. Consequently he came up with the idea of "dog show jumping," not exactly a new idea as there had been earlier displays of dogs jumping obstacles.

But for Crufts John Varley needed the help of people who knew what agility, as it later became known, was all about. A group in the Lincoln area, led by Peter Meanwell, now a General Committee member, built equipment and it was decided two teams should compete at Crufts, 1978, which then was still at Olympia. The event proved immensely popular and in the next year, again at Crufts, three teams took part.

Crufts moved in 1981 from Olympia to Earls Court and for two years, 1981 and 1982, agility was suspended. In 1991 Crufts moved again, to the National Exhibition Centre, Birmingham, with agility by now well established.

The last year at Olympia, 1980, coincided with the introduction of the new Kennel Club Agility Regulations. Gradually, with the passing of the years, agility was taken more as a serious sport than an entertaining demonstration and now has thousands of enthusiasts world-wide. So great is its popularity that in 1999 the General Committee of the Kennel Club discussed and approved the idea of a championship and moves are being made to formulate rules and regulations.

Bernard Hall

'Casey Joes' built on firm foundation

I *BEGAN to wonder* why there wasn't a junior organisation in dogs, comparable to the Pony Club in horses. Something to give an active interest in shows but also an involvement away from the show scene; an opportunity for youngsters to gain an all round knowledge of dogs'.

So thought Mrs. Daphne MacDougall in the latter part of the 1970's. Her late husband, John MacDougall became chairman of the Kennel Club in 1981, and when she discussed the possibility of an organisation being formed, his reply was, 'Well work it out, make some notes and we will see how we go from there.'

She drew up an outline of how she imagined an organisation might take shape, what items of practical interest would be popular and appeal to young people, and then developed a framework of what should be the aims of a junior organisation.

She comments that 'when all the various difficulties were brought to my attention by senior Kennel Club people I did have my doubts as to whether the idea would ever get off the ground. My husband was a tremendous help as he had an idea what would be acceptable to the Kennel Club and what was possible to implement. I was thrilled by the enthusiasm and encouragement of those who supported it, and eventually, with a great deal of patience and persuasion, the Kennel Club Junior Organisation came to fruition.'

The General Committee approved the concept and at the Bi-annual General Meeting in November, 1984, the members voted in favour, and Mrs. Macdougalls' dream took on a positive form.

By January 1985, much background work had been undertaken and, most importantly, an enormous amount of enthusiasm had been engendered. By March, 1985, the framework was set and approved. The organisation was to be called The Kennel Club Junior Organisation. Abbreviated to K.C.J.O., it didn't take long for some to refer to the members as 'Casey Joes'

The aims and objectives of the organisation were:-

• To encourage young people to take an interest in the care and training of dogs, and to enjoy all activities connected with dogs.

• To promote courtesy, sportsmanship, loyalty and self discipline

• To develop a sense of responsibility in canine activities.

To serve the whole country, and ensure an efficient management structure the K.C.J.O. was divided into eight regions, run by a council appointed by the General Committee of the Kennel Club. Each region was to be responsible for organising its own detailed activities, with a number of national competitions to be run each year involving representatives from all the regions.

Weston Park Triathlon Runner Up with Mrs Daphne MacDougall, whose idea the Kennel Club Junior Organisation was.

The first regional organisers were invited - Scotland to be represented by Mr J Aitken Johnston, Wales by Mr Graham Hill and Northern Ireland by Mrs Joyce Crawford. In England, the North-West & the Isle of Man were represented by Mrs Hilda Parkinson, the North East by Mr. Neville Perkins, South and South West by Mrs Angela Cavill, South East by Miss Sally Kimber, and the Midlands by Mrs. Meriel Hathaway. The disciplines of obedience and agility were to be co-ordinated by Mrs. C. C. Guard.

Mr John MacDougall (right) and Brig. Alec Campbell.

Initially, for the first three years, the chairman and the vice-chairman of The Kennel Club General Committee, Mr John MacDougall and Brigadier Alec Campbell, were to form part of the council. However their intention was not to remain once the project was firmly launched.

Without doubt, the wisdom and guidance of these two did much to ensure the sound foundation and the consequent success of the organisation. It says a great deal, that the original framework and the original aims and objectives were so carefully thought out that they remain the same and are as valid now as they were when the organisation was founded in 1985.

A great deal of debate centred on how the aims and objectives could be developed and implemented. It was decided that regions, as well as organising competitive canine activities, would aim to broaden the scope and interest by arranging visits to places of interest such as police dog training centres, Guide Dogs for the Blind, Hearing Dogs for the Deaf, and also arrange instruction on all matters relating to the objectives. Most importantly there should be a framework of rewards for achievements.

The Junior Awards scheme needed to be all embracing to cover every area where members could participate. Members were to keep a log book or diary recording all aspects of their involvement with dogs including such items as kennel management, lectures and discussions, stewarding experience, handling and showing, attendance at dog events, training and experience in judging. Rewards for achievement and excellence would be presented at Crufts.

A national quiz was organised, regional teams were selected to compete with the two successful teams going forward to a final.

The support of central administration was to be provided by the Kennel Club. Miss Wendy Johnson, who worked in the press office and was well known for her part in the elegant presentations in the main ring at Crufts, was appointed as membership secretary.

It was decided that Crufts 1985 would be the ideal time and place for the official launch of this new venture. Probably the proudest

member at that Crufts was Fiona Lilburn of Swansea. The first competition had been to design a logo for the membership badge and Fiona was the winner. Her prize was to be a V.I.P. guest of the Kennel Club at Crufts, which was a memorable day for her, but it must be a source of even greater pleasure and pride to see the badge she designed being worn by today's membership.

The council worked long and hard to consider a range of activities which would appeal to members and fulfil the aims of the organisation. "Showing" was high on the agenda, and it seemed logical to devise a class where youngsters were in competition between themselves and not with adults. As a preliminary step, a stakes class specifically for K.C.J.O. members was drawn up with the intention that the member should be responsible for the care and preparation of the dog. The rules were quite specific. The dog must be owned by the member or the member's family, meaning that the dog should live under the same roof as the member. It was to be a class where the dogs were judged on merit and not merely a handling class.

Registered societies were approached and asked to schedule the class, and it was also requested that consideration could be given to appointing K.C.J.O. members as trainee stewards. The Scottish and Welsh Kennel Clubs were wholehearted in their support, as were Belfast, Blackpool, Leeds, Southern Counties, Birmingham National and Birmingham City Championship Shows.

May 1985, saw the first K.C.J.O. rally. It was sponsored by Birmingham Dog Show Society, organisers of 'the National', and the J. Arthur Rank suite at Stoneleigh was booked and the programme arranged.

Pedigree Petfoods sponsored the event and the organisers nervously awaited what it was hoped would attract an influx of interested youngsters. In total 85 attended over the two days and 30 new members were enrolled. It is interesting and rewarding to see how some of those early members have progressed in the dog world; among them were Sarah Swigiski, now no stranger to handling American Cocker Spaniels at the highest level; Edward and Richard Allen with Richard often seen handling terriers to group and best in show level; Nicola Spencer who not only went on to win in adult competition in the show ring, but also made her mark helping Hilda Parkinson with the organisation in the North-West region. The obedience demonstration by Angela Richmond and Limelight sparked off an interest and enthusiasm for obedience, a new discipline for many members.

Following this more and more championship and open shows scheduled classes, with many of the championship shows also offering facilities to hold rallies. The infectious enthusiasm of C.C. Guard was very much the driving force behind agility and obedience.

The council was given a deadline that at Crufts, 1986, there WOULD be a regional obedience competition and an agility grand prix. Under C.C.'s driving tuition, we learned 'fast track'. Detailed rules for an obedience certificate were approved and she had the foresight to appreciate the attraction of obedience being a team event with the team finals being contested at Crufts.

Before long, most regions were fielding competent teams. Initially, most of the dogs were of the working Collie type, but a few enthusiasts appreciated that other breeds were capable of working obedience. With the encouragement of Angela Richmond and the example of her Golden Retriever, the then Ob. Ch. Melfricka Limelight, Greg Wythnall, in the Midlands, started to train his Golden Retriever Fern, and made their performances and success into something of a leader and a legend.

By 1987 there was a need to have separate levels of competition, so not only a basic, but also a test of advanced obedience were developed. More recently, in response to popular demand by the members, an intermediate level has been introduced.

Agility was already popular in the adult world, and this seemed to be a discipline which would appeal to youngsters. Having structured the rules for members to win a certificate in agility, a grand final was to involve every youngster who gained a certificate. The City of Birmingham championship show (which co-incided with school holidays) agreed to host the final.

Popular? Just how popular no one imagined. All age groups, with all sorts, shapes and sizes of dogs competed. To make a manageable competition, this necessitated the qualifiers being split into four sections. Youngsters were in age groups eight to 11, 12 to 14, 16 to 18,with a separate class for "mini" dogs.

Currently, with upwards of 100 members qualifying, the event at Birmingham is now a semi-final, and to bring it into line with other events, the K.C.J.O. Agility Dog of the Year final is held at Crufts.

The Quiz, initially organised by Angela Cavill, is held at regional events throughout the year. Questions relate to dogs and any variety of canine matters. Regional organisers select teams consisting of one member from each age group, plus a team captain. From inter-regional competition the two top teams then go forward to a grand final. With most youngsters now being so involved and busy at Crufts, this final is no longer held there, but is a separate event. The two winning teams battle it out in the Board Room of the Kennel Club, under the watchful eyes of the portrait of Mr MacDougall.

As well as planning national events, much work went on in the regions. The distinctive K.C.J.O. flag was seen flying at many championship shows where accommodation was provided. In those early days most regions held rallies and seminars, a variety of activities arranged to interest members, ranging from photographic and essay competitions, to 'fun' days. Events raising money for charities were organised by K.C.J.O. members under the supervision of their regional organiser.

Angela Richmond and her Golden Retriever, Ob.Ch. Melfricka Limelight, who between them did so much to encourage obedience in the KCJO movement. She is seen being presented with her second obedience challenge certificate by Joan Lavender in 1986.

The support for the 'Casey Joes' and their activities was increasing,and plans were made for their involvement at Crufts 1986.

Sir Dudley Forwood, then chairman of Crufts, made a 'club' room available for K.C.J.O. members. There was a display illustrating all the activities undertaken by the organisation, with a calendar of regional events.

Special emphasis was placed on those events which would culminate in final competition at Crufts, 1987.

A birthday cake was baked to celebrate the first anniversary of the K.C.J.O. In a formal ceremony, every day of the show, a celebrity cut a birthday cake.

Crufts was an ideal high profile platform to further objectives, by giving members an environment to take part in finals competitions, and an opportunity to generate new members, to promote the aims of the organisation and to raise its profile with the canine world, the general public and the media.

Melissa Allen with her Miniature Schnauzer, Kaston Tudor Night. Melissa was first in the Mini Class of the KCJO Agility Dog of the Year Competition 1996.

These young people were found to be responsible and valuable 'team' players at Crufts. They were involved as 'scouts' assisting group stewards and exhibitors early in the morning at the entrance gates; assisting in the Crufts office, gathering best of breed results for the press office. They assisted regional organisers in administration and presentation of events held in the special events ring. In 1993 and 1994, the stylish guard of honour for the best in show spectacle in the main ring was formed by K.C.J.O. members. By the tenth anniversary of the organisation in 1995, members were involved in the Good Citizen Dog Scheme first aid and grooming demonstrations. Trainee stewards were used in the obedience rings and two of these have now progressed to judging. Jason Wood and Lucy Doughty have actually judged junior obedience at Crufts. Trainee stewards are now being used in breed rings and these young people are undertaking a wide range of activities in a most responsible manner.

Few people are aware of the amount of practice involved to achieve the split-second timing which ensures the live world-wide television coverage of Crufts Best in Show. On the Friday and Saturday nights of the show, seven K.C.J.O. members with their dogs, act as 'stand-ins' for the group winners at the television "dress" rehearsals. Along with the Best in Show judge and the enormous team which achieves the perfection of this spectacular event, they rehearse until each detail is as near perfect as possible. The youngsters have the thrill of the B.I.S. judge selecting two of their dogs as

winner and runner up. They also work as part of a team and endure the discipline of working as long as it takes to achieve perfection.

That first presence of the K.C.J.O. at Crufts in 1986,was successful in raising an overall awareness of their organisation and K.C.J.O. members became familiar figures at many national events. Dressed in their distinctive green track suits, they undertook a multitude of activities.

No organisation stands still if it is to succeed, and the K.C.J.O. is no exception. As the organisation progressed, so did a change in members' interests. With more opportunity for their involvement at shows, members had less time for seminars and lectures. As attendance and interest decreased 'hospitality' areas were created with educational talks being held as separate events in the regions.

Consideration needed to be given to include and provide activities for youngsters with non pedigree dogs and for those members who, although interested in dogs, were unable to own a dog of their own. One such was the National Great Dog Walk of 1988. Each region arranged a sponsored walk, and a grand total of £3,080 was raised by the K.C.J.O. Other events to raise money for approved charities were organised by individuals in the regions, among them Rachel Callows' obedience and agility show which raised £500 for Guide Dogs for the Blind; Claire Shaw's exemption show which raised £280 for muscular dystrophy; Birmingham Children's Hospice received £500 from an exemption show organised by Midlands members.

In 1992, Mrs MacDougall put forward another of her ideas - that there should be a competition to show that 'beautiful' dogs can have brains, and the triathlon event was devised. It had trial runs at the Midlands region major event held in conjunction with the Pony Club Championships at Weston Park, Shropshire. The competition comprised three sections, 'beauty' to be assessed as a breed stakes class; obedience and agility. Each section was judged and marked with the competitor having the highest total overall mark being the winner. Mr. and Mrs. MacDougall watched with enthusiasm, and agreed this would make a good regional event, leading to a demonstration at Crufts. By 1996 there was sufficient regional interest to support national exposure at Crufts.

Anyone present at that first demonstration will remember Mr. MacDougalls' delight when the American Cocker Spaniel made it quite obvious that obedience and agility were not that appealing, and decided to leave the ring. The crowd loved that little character dog and what support they gave the youngsters and their dogs who were pioneering what has now become a popular and polished competition.

As the triathlon became part of the programme for pedigree dogs Catherine Fuller, a member, asked the council whether it would be possible to devise a competition for non-pedigree dogs, and so the biathlon was structured. This competition tests obedience and agility, and any dog, provided it is on the Kennel Club Working Trials, Obedience or Breed register, is eligible to compete. The winner is the competitor gaining highest total marks overall.

There was an interest in and a demand from members for their own show handling competition. There was already a Junior Handling Association, founded by Joe Cartledge, a talented dog handler, a true 'dog man', with great interest in training and encouraging youth. After his death Mrs. Liz Cartledge continued to organise what has now developed into a highly popular international association.

The K.C.J.O. handling competition places emphasis on the handler's knowledge of the breed being handled, with an awareness of how the dog compares with the breed standard. The dog should be handled as it would be in the show ring.

Each region now holds an annual competition to select winning handlers in the three age groups, and regional teams compete at Crufts to determine the overall individual and team winners. The individual winner, K.C.J.O. Handler of the Year, goes forward to represent the United Kingdom in the International Junior Show Handler of the Year final held on the last day of Crufts.

K.C.J.O. regional handling finalists undergo an obligatory theoretical assessment. Before the practical competition, each competitor has an oral examination to assess overall knowledge and understanding of the preparation, presentation and care of the dog; the methods and reasons for handling an individual dog and different breeds. In fact this demonstrates depth of understanding of what makes for a successful handler in the show ring. This is a important section of the K.C.J.O. handling competition, and the winner is awarded a separate 'Question Time' trophy, which is presented in the K.C.J.O. ring.

A 'Casey Joe' works his dog through the weaving poles at a KCJO camp agility contest.

Another milestone in the development of K.C.J.O. was in 1991 when Eric Smethurst then chairman, suggested a summer camp. Council set out that such a camp should provide members with a holiday, with learning experience of most dog disciplines while enjoying the company of other juniors from various areas of the country. The suggested format was that camp should cover a period of one week, there should be camping facilities, and it should cater for specialised training and social activities. Members would be encouraged to participate in the organisation of the camp and its events.

The first camp in August 1992, was at a girls' residential school in Cobham, Surrey, with extensive, private, secure grounds, residential as well as camping facilities, and of course, sports facilities. The enthusiasm of C.C. Guard and Sally Kimber who organised the camp, those regional organisers who attended, parents, and particularly the youngsters, made this venture an unqualified success. Mr. and Mrs. MacDougall and a few of the General Committee visited and were impressed by the range of training and the youngsters' obvious enjoyment. The camp is now a major event in the calendar, a massive administrative undertaking, a week of concentrated mental and physical effort which is quite exhausting for

*Adrian Marrett, KCJO
Junior of the Year 1999,
being presented with the
Shaun McAlpine Trophy
by HRH Prince Michael
of Kent at Crufts 1999.*

members and totally exhausting for organisers. But it is also very rewarding and worthwhile. To help attendance from all regions the camp moves around the country and to date, has been in Surrey, Derbyshire, Gloucestershire, Shropshire and Yorkshire.

Neville Perkins, first organiser of the North-East region, devised a points system and awards books for stewarding and showing. The books are signed by judges or stewards to confirm the youngsters' wins which qualify for cloth badges which are worn with great pride. Metal badges and bars are awarded to the highest achievers. Those who pass the stewarding test receive both a certificate and a metal bar. In true Olympic style, gold, silver and bronze medals are presented at Crufts to top winners in obedience, agility, handling, stakes and Junior of the Year competitions. To win a trophy is a great achievement,but the history associated with some of the K.C.J.O. trophies, makes them very special indeed.

The Shaun McAlpine Memorial Trophy was donated in 1985, and presented to the K.C.J.O. at Crufts 1986. It is an antique French bronze model of a Great Dane, dated about 1860. Shaun McAlpine made a great impact as a youngster, with his sportsmanship and dedication and achieved great success in the show ring with his Great Danes. His professional, determined attitude, his presentation of self and dog, his empathy with

all the dogs he handled, his modesty in success, made him a role model for young and old alike. After his tragic death, his parents asked that the trophy should be presented on an annual basis to a member of the K.C.J.O. who had made a significant contribution to the canine world and played a major part in a number of canine activities.

This special trophy is awarded to the winner of the Junior of the Year competition, and is presented at Crufts by H.R.H. Prince Michael of Kent, who also presents a gold medal to the overall winner, plus silver and bronze medals to the winners in the other age groups.

The Evergreen Princess Trophy, a model of a Golden Retriever, is presented to the winning team in the advanced obedience competition. Donated by Greg Wythnall in memory of his Golden Retriever Fern, it is a reminder of the wonderful partnership and achievement of Greg and Fern in the early days of the K.C.J.O.

The Silver Salver awarded to the K.C.J.O. Handler of the Year was presented by a former chairman, Bill Wadman Taylor (a trophy awarded to the winning region in the competition was donated by The Dogs Home, Battersea where Mr. Wadman Taylor had worked) The winner of the important theoretical section of the competition receives the 'Question Time' trophy, donated by Mr. David and Mrs. Angela Cavill.

H.S.H. Princess Antoinette of Monaco annually donates a memento for the winner of the K.C.J.O. stakes final, who also receives the Stewton Cup. The runner up receives the Ivanhoe Cup, a trophy originally owned by the Newport Show and dated 1891. The winner of the Agility Dog of the Year competition receives a silver cup dated 1906, donated by the Birmingham Dog Show Society.

In obedience, the junior gaining most points over the year receives the Rebecca Pointer Memorial Trophy. This bronze model of a sheepdog, is donated in memory of John Purton and his dog Farmers Lark, who did so much to help young people in obedience, and is presented to the winner of the advanced obedience.

The Lady Zena of Zephyr trophy was donated by Emma Jones, a K.C.J.O. member and is awarded to the highest placed dog of a breed other than a Border Collie, in the test of obedience.

The two most recently donated trophies have a very particular and special history. On the death of Mr. MacDougall, Mr. John Spurling asked that he be allowed to donate a memorial trophy. This very splendid John MacDougall Quaich is presented to the winner of the triathlon competition. Mr. Spurling also donates a small replica of the Quaich which the lucky winner keeps as a permanent memento.

The biathlon, with its emphasis on obedience and agility, would have been a competition dear to the heart of Brig. Campbell. A bequest from him enabled a trophy to be purchased and is awarded annually to the winner of the biathlon. Brig. Campbell was the first chairman of the K.C.J.O. and when interviewed at the inception of the organisation he referred to his previous involvement with the training of young people while commandant of the Army Apprentice School in Jersey.

He said "We had some 30 boys from all walks of life. I soon recognised how boys could be encouraged to work and play with real enthusiasm and little or no resort to military discipline. Plenty of honest 'one upmanship' went into trying to make sure Campbell house won quite a lot! Looking back with pride, we can claim to have produced, yes from the ranks, a general, one brigadier, two colonels and 30 captains and majors. I sincerely hope that our

Junior Organisation will encourage and impart 'knowhow' to young people from every walk of life provided they are interested in dogs, keen to learn more, and work hard."

Brig. Campbell's primary interest in dogs was an attraction to working trials and obedience. He had worked three German Shepherd Dogs and brought to the K.C.J.O. a depth of knowledge of the interests and motivation of young people and enormous enthusiasm and determination to make the K.C.J.O. a success. On his retirement in 1987, he was succeeded by Bill Wadman Taylor, a veterinary surgeon who had a particular interest in Cairn Terriers.

In 1991, Eric Smethurst became chairman. A great 'ideas' man, his period of office saw two major milestones in the development of the organisation; the annual national camp, and the triathlon. From 1993 to the present day, the chairman has been Bill Hardaway, who is the longest serving chairman to date and with special interest in obedience and working trials.

What of the future?

With such a unique organisation in place, it is possible other kennel clubs may become interested in formulating a similar training ground for their young people. There have already been informal visits to the Kennel Club by youngsters from the U.S.A., and hopefully, the future will bring an interchange of ideas of mutual interest and benefit with strong links with other kennel clubs.

The John MacDougall Quaich, awarded annually to the winner of the triathlon.

No organisation exists in isolation, and the K.C.J.O. is no exception to this. There are already links with some Pony Club activities, and hopefully the future will see stronger links with more combined events taking place between the members of these two organisations.

In consultation with the K.C.J.O., the Cub Scouts have introduced an Animal Lovers Badge, and the first packs to qualify for this badge, were presented with their awards in the K.C.J.O. ring at Crufts. This understanding of the care of the dog and interest in responsible animal welfare, will spread to many other youth organisations, in the future.

123

Mr John MacDougall pictured with a KCJO member while presenting prizes for the essay competition,
at Birmingham Dog Show Society 'National' Show.

Who knows what exciting projects lie ahead? It would be naive to expect from a membership which in the year 2000 numbers around 2000, that all will rise to the heights in the dog world. However, we can assume that all members will gain an understanding of responsible dog ownership; will have been encouraged and assisted to discover and develop their full potential in those areas which interest them. Already we are seeing some of the early members taking on high profile roles in show management, competing, judging and training.

The K.C.J.O. must be one of the most precious jewels in the crown of the Kennel Club. The value of any jewel lies in its size but, more importantly, in its quality. The original jewel may have been small but it was of prime quality. Although the future will see an increase in size, it is imperative that the quality is maintained. In this way, the Kennel Club Junior Organisation will continue to be one of the treasures of the Kennel Club.

Meriel Hathaway

London Laughs: Kennel Club
'No. It seems you must have a pedigree.' (Lee)

'I don't want a prize – just get me into a stall next to that little 'Best-in-her-class' Golden Spaniel!' (George Dunnet)

Responsible ownership a lifeline for dogs

*T*HE *Kennel Club has been* developing the message of responsible dog ownership to dog owners and non-dog owners for many years and this can be seen through all walks of life. The message has become a real social lifeline for dogs in Britain and become a public relations prize winner in the Kennel Club's gallery of treasures.

Responsible dog ownership encompasses a wide variety of messages, three of which are CHOICE, CARE and TRAINING. The Kennel Club has developed schemes, strategies and events to ensure that potential and current dog owners are able to become better owners and appreciate the benefits that dogs bring to our lives.

CHOICE

The decision to bring a dog into a home and family life is not one to be made on impulse. The Kennel Club has identified the need for potential dog owners to choose a dog that suits their own lifestyle and situation and provides many services to help the prospective dog owner. One of the first steps to making a decision comes from the Kennel Club's own guide to responsible dog ownership - *The Canine Code,* which provides a starting point for non-dog owners. It encourages them to think before they buy and covers a wide selection of information including the law, insurance, health issues, contacts and social responsibilities. Each year, the Kennel Club publishes over 100,000 copies of the code to assist people in finding out more about choosing the right pet to suit their lifestyle.

The Kennel Club identified that there is also a need for people to be able to interact with many different breeds at an event: this has been achieved through the development of Discover Dogs, a unique event created in 1994 by the Crufts committee. Discover Dogs brings together over 180 breeds of pedigree dog in one area twice a year so that visitors are able to interact with the many different breeds that the

Kennel Club recognises (currently 192). Breed representatives give their time to this event to promote and, on occasions, dissuade people from buying a certain breed. Visitors can find out all the important issues before getting a puppy and ensure that they make the right choice - enabling them to provide the dog with the long term commitment and life they deserve.

The benefits of this concept at Crufts were seen as two fold - firstly to relieve the pressure on exhibitors at Crufts by visitors to the show who wanted to know more about specific breeds and, secondly to provide an educational vehicle for potential dog owners.

Discover Dogs provides visitors with a unique opportunity of meeting over 180 different breeds of dog and learning more about responsible dog ownership.

After three extremely successful years at Crufts it was felt that the demand was so great for this concept that it was decided to launch Discover Dogs also as a stand alone event. Since Crufts had moved to Birmingham in 1991, London was left without a major canine event. The venue for Discover Dogs was chosen as Earls Court, London, and in August 1996 the first Discover Dogs in London was launched.

That first year saw a promising but slow start and with a change of date from summer to the cooler autumn months, the event now attracts over 20,000 visitors, with 1999 achieving the highest London total to date. Discover Dogs also provides visitors with displays and informative stands where they can find out more about canine activities, Kennel Club services, training, charities and more than 80 trade stands, so that even if they already have a pet at home, their relationship can become more rewarding.

CARE

Once someone has chosen the breed of dog with which they are happy, learning how to care for it is the next step. Caring for a pet involves not only providing good exercise and food, but also veterinary care, identification, insurance and, of course, a responsible attitude.

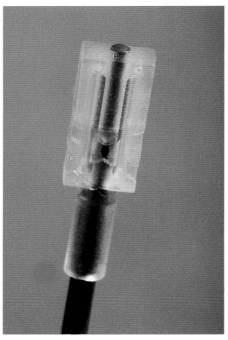

The microchip is implanted under the skin at the base of the neck and once correctly implanted, the chip, which bears a unique registration number, remains for life.

Identification is one of the hot topics for the start of the new millennium. Quarantine has existed in this country since 1901, but the Government has now put forward plans to abolish the six month detention period for cats and dogs coming into this country.

In February , 1999, the Kennel Club was asked to review the Kennedy Report on the reform of the UK quarantine laws. The recommendations on this report were supported by the Kennel Club focusing on identification and vaccination and highlighting the importance of maintaining a rabies free status.

Accurate identification is key to this new 'pet passport' scheme, while also being vital to the safe and speedy return of a lost dog to its owner. Collars and tags have been law for pets in Britain for many years, but, on occasion, this form of identification fails. Microchipping is one form which offers permanent identification. A tiny chip, approximately the size of a rice grain, is implanted under the skin at the base of the neck. Once correctly implanted, the chip, which bears a unique registration number, remains for life.

Microchips are now regularly used to identify animals across the world. The Kennel Club soon realised the importance of identification and in 1995 set up a database with the RSPCA and the Scottish SPCA. The register encompasses all forms of identification including microchipping, collar tags and tattooing. The majority of pets on the database are microchipped and the current database has more than 635,000 dogs, cats and other species and adds over 38,000 new entries each month. Dogs make up more than 70% of the total, illustrating the importance placed by owners on identification.

Pets are microchipped by their veterinary surgeon and details are sent to PetLog, the Kennel Club national pet identification scheme for entry on to the database. Once entered, the information is available, through computer access, to local authorities, police and established welfare and rescue organisations when a lost pet is found. The service provides peace of mind for the owner and ensures that lost or stray animals are quickly reunited with their owners.

The Kennel Club promotes the importance of identification whenever possible, but it does not believe that this should lead to compulsory registration of dogs. At present there are laws and bylaws to cover all aspects of irresponsible dog ownership whether it be dog fighting, dangerous dogs or fouling. The education of the irresponsible dog owner will not be achieved by further legislation or registration.

The care and understanding of dogs is of vital importance, not only can the relationship between dog and human develop, but it can be one of the most rewarding processes that lasts for many years.

TRAINING

A trained dog is a happy dog. The Kennel Club's Good Citizen Dog Scheme is the epitome of responsible dog ownership. First developed in 1992 to promote a more responsible and caring attitude towards dogs in our society, the scheme has grown rapidly.

In 1992 it was introduced to dog training clubs throughout Britain and to date 35,000 dogs and their owners have successfully passed the course through over 1,000 training clubs, local councils, adult education centres and agricultural colleges.

The general public's perception of dogs is an issue that is continually addressed by the Kennel Club. Given there is concern about such matters as dog fouling and uncontrolled dogs which may cause nuisance through noise or aggression, this scheme was specifically established to promote responsible ownership. A well trained dog is both socially acceptable and a joy to the owner and such dogs are much less likely to cause complaint.

The scheme is divided into three parts - bronze, silver and gold. The bronze level has been in place since the scheme started in 1992 and silver and gold were launched in May, 1998. The constituent parts of each are:

Bronze: 1) Cleanliness and identification 2) Collar and lead 3) Walk on lead 4) Control at door/gate 5) Controlled walk through people and dogs 6) Stay down on lead 7) Grooming the dog (8) Present for examination 9) Return to the handler

Silver: 1) Play with the dog 2) Road walk 3) Rejoin the handler 4) Stay in one place 5) Vehicle control 6) Come away from distractions 7) Controlled greeting 8) Food manners (9) Examination of the dog 10) Responsibility and care

Gold: 1) Road walk 2) Return to handler's side 3) Walk free beside handler 4) Stay down in one place 5) Send the dog to bed 6) Stop the dog 7) Relaxed isolation 8) Food manners 9) Responsibility and care

All three Good Citizen levels have a responsibility and care section which has been put in place so that the owner can show they have a good knowledge of dog ownership and they are tested on questions of identification, vaccination, the law that relates to dogs and other matters.

This scheme has become a phenomenal success and a bench mark for canine social behaviour. Dog shows from exemption to championship level, dog wardens, charities, events, further education establishments and schools have embraced the scheme as their own. The scheme is for all dogs, both cross-bred and pedigree, young or old and is non-competitive.

A good citizen dog is a joy to live with and an ideal dog to own. The Kennel Club sees the scheme as providing dog owners with a training programme that really can make a difference to their lives.

The Kennel Club has promoted the importance of education in this country and has become a pioneer in promoting responsible dog ownership across the world. Through the introduction and development of these schemes, it is hoped that humans and dogs alike can continue to live in harmony.

Helen Pollitt

Pointer, 1905 – Arthur Wardle.

Acknowledgments

The co-editors and authors wish to acknowledge the invaluable help given by many people in the research of this book, not least Kennel Club staff of many departments and especially Barbara Walker and Rebecca Cantwell of the library; Kennel Club Members, especially Dennis Ashley, Stan Ford, Len Hammond, Bill Hardaway, Harry Hardwicke, Daphne MacDougall, Leonarda Pogodzinski, Chris Seidler, John Williams and Warwick Winston.

Joyce Adams, Lucinda Aldrich-Blake, Anne Chadwick, Peter Embling, Mary Girling, Peggy Grayson, Edward Horswell, (The Slademore Gallery, London), Clifford L B Hubbard, Joan Lavender, Brian Leonard, Nigel Massey, Tan Nagrecha, Dr Desiree Scott, William Secord (William Secord Gallery Inc., New York), Peter Winfield and Dog World Publications Ltd.

Photographs

Photographs have been contributed to this book from many sources, especially those listed below whose work is not separately credited:

	Page
Hartley Campbell	2
Matthew Carr	111(1)
C M Cooke	72(L), 73(L)
Prudence Cuming Associates Ltd.	3(1), 6–53, 56–67, 69, 70, 72(R), 74, 75, 76, 83, 86 (cartoon), 88, 90, 91, 96, 98, 99, 101–104, 109, 110, 124 (cartoons), 127, 130
David Dalton	84
Dog World Photographic Library	85, 107, 112(2)
Thomas Fall	106(R)
Frank Garwood/Dog World	73(R)
John Hartley	92, 112(5)
Peter Heard	113–115
Marc Henrie	iv, 54, 68, 112(1, 3, 4),116(R), 122, 126
Chris Labina	125
David Lindsay	120
Andrew Martin Photography	86
William Moores	3(2)
Godfrey New Photographers	1
The Press Association Ltd.	108
Dave Ray	116(L)
Royal Photograph Collection	106(L)
Lucie Sear	111(2)
Scott Wills Design	4

Works of Reference

American Kennel Gazette

Edward C Ash. *Dogs: Their History and Development*

E Benezit. *Dictionnaire Des Peintres, Sculpteurs, Dessinateurs et Graveurs*

Holland Buckley. *The Airedale Terrier*

Winifred E Chadwick. *The Borzoi Handbook*

Herbert Compton. *The Twentieth Century Dog*

Robert E Heal. *Bill Siggers: He Whacked the Bloody Lot*

Walter Hutchinson (Editor). *Hutchinson's Dog Encyclopaedia*

Lilla Ives. *Show Pomeranians*

Edward William Jaquet. *The Kennel Club, a History and Record of its Work, London 1905*

Adrian Jones. *Memoirs of a Soldier Artist*

J Johnson & A Greutzner (Compilers). *The Dictionary of British Artists 1880-1940*

Kennel Club. *Kennel Gazettes*

Kennel Club. *Kennel Club Stud Books*

Marion Keyte-Perry. *The Samoyed*

Robert Leighton. *The New Book of the Dog*

Henry Mayhew. *London Labour and the London Poor*

John T Marvin. *The Fox Terrier Scrapbook*

Richard Ormond. *Sir Edwin Landseer*

Christopher Payne. *Animals in Bronze*

Sidney H Paviere. *A Dictionary of British Sporting Painters*

Pure Bred Dogs

Samuel Redgrave. *A Dictionary of Artists of the English School*

Francis Henry Salvin & William Brodrick. *Falconry in the British Isles*

William Secord. *Dog Painting 1840-1940*

Dr Desiree Scott. *A Celebration of Crufts*

Vero Shaw. *The Illustrated Book of the Dog*

C H Douglas Todd. *The Popular Whippet*

Who's Who.

Mary Ann Wingfield. *A Dictionary of Sporting Artists 1650-1990*

Christopher Wood. *The Dictionary of Victorian Painters*

Veronica Tudor Williams. *Basenjis the Barkless Dog*

Veronica Tudor Williams. *Fula Basenji from the Jungle*

Foxhounds

Field Spaniel

Hanging on the walls of the stairway at the Kennel Club are a number of fascinating sketches by Maud Earl. A selection are reproduced here.

Greyhounds

Clumber Spaniels